OFFICE ARCADE

JASON SURIANO

OFFICE ARCADE

GAMIFICATION, BYTE SIZE LEARNING, AND OTHER WINS ON THE WAY TO PRODUCTIVE HUMAN RESOURCES

LIONCREST
PUBLISHING

OFFICE ARCADE
*Gamification, Byte-Size Learning, and Other Wins
on the Way to More Productive Human Resources*

ISBN   978-1-61961-605-9 *Paperback*
       978-1-61961-606-6 *Ebook*

For Jennifer, Ethan, and Malcolm

CONTENTS

——

| gām-if-i-cāSH-en | noun

*the use of design and insights from video
games in the organizational space to engage
trainees on multiple devices as they follow
a learning narrative to targeted outcomes,
generating real-time assessment data*

CHAPTER 1

BREAKING THE EXPECTATION BARRIER

Let's face it: too much in the human resources management and training arena is stuck in neutral. Beliefs like "people can only learn so fast," and "time equals learning," and "tests *should* be hard" have lulled too many HR and training professionals into complacency about what can be accomplished and have impoverished the business case for their roles in their organizations. It's no wonder so many find their organizational status under attack and their budgets being eroded.

If this were a video game, it would be about time for HR to discover a handy superpower.

Well, guess what: technology and the practical understanding of human motivation have moved on. And they've done it in a place you might least expect—in the escapist worlds of first arcade and then computer-based gaming.

By bringing insights from the $100 billion computer and online gaming industry into the office, the techniques I describe in this book break the expectations that have blocked real advances in training and human resources productivity until now. They may even be the first real breakthrough in corporate and organizational training since the invention of the video link.

The insights I'll share here fundamentally change the dynamic of organizational training and assessment, from one of supervisory "push"—and some "shove"—to eager employee "pull." They do away with much of the anxiety that impedes traditional learning and distorts conventional assessment scores. They leverage learners' willing engagement to shorten the time to targeted training goals and enhance content retention.

Because all this happens in an on-demand environment, these methods provide continuous, real-time feedback on learners' progress. This unprecedented level of data generates a far richer body of human resources and operational insight than any previous training approach at this level of investment can deliver.

This approach—gamified learning, training, and assessment—delivers instructional and HR professionals powerful new tools to do what they've always done best even better. What's even more exciting is that it provides those professionals with compelling new deliverables that strongly support the business case for their unique value within their organizations.

But it's not all play and win. To take advantage of these tools and insights, HR and training professionals need to up their games, too. Gamified learning leverages how today's generation engages with the world, as well as how it escapes from it into entertainment. Securing that engagement requires suspending some old habits and beliefs—and ditching some twentieth-century modes of communication. Say good-bye to paper binders once and for all, and also to stale PowerPoint documents and e-learning tools that simply slap the same dry information up onto a laptop screen.

Gamification—I know, it's a mouthful—isn't a new coat of technology slapped on the same old awareness training, onboarding, and credential-maintenance material. Over the last decade and a half, it has radically rethought how people learn best. And it has proven those concepts in real-world products that maximize learners' receptivity and document their accomplishing of targeted outcomes. It takes a new approach to delivering content in "byte-size" knowledge morsels, served up in a narrative context that engages people's natural interests.

And the rethink is coming just in time. The training and HR game is changing—fast. Upcoming generations are not only digital natives, but increasingly they're also app-native in the way they engage new information. They want it when they need it, not before. And they're restless, moving constantly among real and virtual tasks, grabbing app time as it suits their priorities and schedules. With the arrival of these entrants into the workforce, organizational trainers and personnel managers face new audiences for whom a game-like environment is not just preferred: it's expected—and increasingly, demanded.

WINNERS IN THE TRAINING GAME

The winners of this new game in the training space will be those human resources professionals who learn and apply these keys to better productivity in their workplace mission. During my decade and a half developing learning and awareness products for clients across North America, I've found that individuals who seize the benefits of gamification get more satisfaction in the creative elements of their work and earn a more valued profile in their organizations.

So, let's get more specific about the benefits companies have reaped once they've learned and applied gamification techniques:

- A vehicle-fleet company tested its best drivers on a gamified HR applicant test—recording performance benchmarks that later allowed managers not only to hire just those individuals who best fit the workplace needs, but even identify those *who might be underutilized in a frontline role.*

- When an infrastructure enterprise with 7,000 employees worldwide gamified its utility division's new employee onboarding process and material, it was amazed to find that 80 percent of new hires had completed company and benefits familiarization *before they even walked in the door on their first day.*

- A professional association used to struggle to ensure that its nearly 50,000 members fulfilled a legal mandate to be up on current statutory changes affecting them. After it gamified what used to be a five-hour open-book exam on this tedious legal material, it discovered its members were completing the work in less than half the time, and doing so *before and after their paid working hours.*

🔴 An environmental services company employed a large number of immigrant and low-reading-skilled workers—and then relied on text-based manuals to teach them about on-site safety. Gamified training put the employees into a real-world scene, where they quickly began to spot the hazards—and *reduced the company's risk of liability and lost time.*

As those examples show, gamified human resources and training engagements pay off—for employees, organizations, and managers.

More enthusiastic employees engage more fully with training and other mandated awareness material. That extra engagement translates into greater knowledge absorption and retention, which in turn improves job performance. It also makes for generally happier, more productive employees. Some organizations have found that their target employees get *so* enthused and engaged, in fact, that they actually *dedicate their own unpaid time* to absorb mandated content.

Learners who eagerly embrace new skills or awareness content are also those who are most likely to apply that knowledge in the workplace. The benefits to their organizations can be as wide-ranging as having fewer lost-time accidents on the job site, branch-office employees getting enthusiastically behind a new head-office strategy, or bumping up the level of new managers' supervisory skills.

And the live, real-time nature of online gamified learning has yet another advantage for trainers and HR professionals. Traditional paper-based assessments reveal a summary of an individual's right and wrong answers on a particular day. But those results are often distorted by anxiety over taking a test. Assessments within gamified environments reduce that anxiety—and the associated distortion in results.

The full capabilities of gamification have come into their own with the extension of the cloud—the presence of Internet connectivity via Wi-Fi or cell data—to more and more public and private spaces. It is this nearly ubiquitous presence that allows gamified training to break out of the office box and enter learners' daily lives in more meaningful exchanges.

It's also what makes a gamified training module almost infinitely scalable at minimal marginal cost. That's a huge advantage when your organization runs to tens of thousands of employees or clients.

Continuous cloud connectivity also allows gamification software to collect durable, time-stamped data on participants' progress through a training module. Where did they pause to think? Where did they stop and go back to review resource material? Where did they get frustrated and just drop out?

This new dimension of available real-time detail at both the individual and workforce scales supports far more finely grained distinctions about the capabilities of new applicants and current personnel than ever before possible outside a $130 million flight simulator. The additional insight allows managers to be more effective, more productive, and more valuable to their organizations.

THE TIME IS NOW

All these advantages are becoming more critical to training and HR professionals every day. Many of my clients in those fields face budget pressures from executive committees that don't feel they're getting organizational value—let alone *growing* value—in HR spending. Others pale at the flood of new technologies that promise to improve their lives. Instead, they just feel overwhelmed by the huge number of choices, and the unavoidable uncertainty about which one will be the magic bullet to make their job easier or more productive.

I'll be honest: there are no magic bullets. Later on, I'll get into what it takes for managers in the human resources space to deploy true gamification techniques the right way in order to reap their incredible advantages to the fullest.

For now, I'll just say this because it's really, really important: even if you're not entirely sold yet on the compelling advantages of gamified learning, your workforce already is.

Today's Millennials and tomorrow's Generation Zers are digital natives accustomed to absorbing the vast majority of what interests them in digital, visual, interactive form. Dead trees in three-ring-binders don't speak their language. Passively staring at overloaded PowerPoint slides doesn't either. A Millennial who goes through the grueling hiring process to join a forward-looking or leading-edge organization, only to be handed a dog-eared binder of benefits and policies on day one and told to sit down and read it, will probably be out the door before lunch.

It's true of all social advances: any time a new technology transforms a work process, there are those who leap and stretch to grasp it—and those who find reasons to resist it. History is pretty clear about how those choices work out. It may take a personal stretch, but the human resources winners of the decades ahead will be the people who are ready to become the builders and keepers of learning games.

CHAPTER 2

JUST PLAYING GAMES?

I hear a lot of objections that gamified learning can't be serious. Seriously? What if I told you that in fact it can pack just as much serious content into less of a trainee's time, who will learn it more willingly—even enthusiastically—without usually even being aware of how much more he's learning?

It's true. And it's one of a number of common misunderstandings that are keeping more professionals in the human resources and training space from grasping and applying the huge benefits available through gamification.

Take the case of a health-provider organization that hired my company for what could be described as a somewhat unusual challenge in onboarding.

The group was a professional body governing the practice of midwives in a North American jurisdiction. Their basic task was to bring trained midwives coming from other countries up to speed on practices here, in order for them to become certified to work.

Making sure these medically qualified midwives were competent professionals was only part of it, though. The organization also needed to familiarize them with nonmedical differences in the North American work culture—for example, the fact that here most midwives attend mothers at their homes, not in a clinic or hospital setting.

The caregivers needed to know their stuff. Lives were at stake. And the association that would be signing off on their readiness needed to *know* they knew it. The client was concerned that nothing important get lost in gamifying their preparation.

Then we showed the client committee that was working with us one of our training modules for the first time. One of the committee members spoke up. She objected that what she saw on the screen didn't look "academically rigorous enough" to be really serious. She didn't think it could possibly convey all the information that people entering the profession needed to know.

This group was planning on giving candidates an examination at the end of this part of their training. I asked the concerned client how many questions would likely be on that exam. "It might be 100 to 125 questions," she said.

I looked at the screen. There were, along with some other images in the background, seven visible action icons or gamified tasks. "Do you realize," I asked her, "that there are eight questions behind each one of those icons? That's 56 questions in that one chapter, and there are eight chapters in the module." That's nearly 450 questions. I call that a lot more rigorous than a 125-question exam.

Some people who aren't yet familiar with the power of gamification and who look at an activity screen can find that the image can look simple. They don't see a lot of dropdown menus or in-your-face text. What they often don't realize is that all the content is still in there. It's just hidden from view until the moment a learner needs or wants it. That doesn't mean the whole experience is less rigorous. It may even be more so. It's just more enjoyable. Is that a bad thing? I happen to think it makes a trainee more eager to learn.

LEARNING SHOULDN'T HURT

I run into the same thing with the length of time that trainers expect a particular lesson to take. Just because it's always taken five hours to deliver some material in the past, doesn't mean it has to be that way forever.

Printed text on paper imposes its own minimum time requirement to read. So does a rudimentary e-learning program that just puts the same text on a screen and asks the user to "click for more" instead of turning the page. Assuming those limitations can't be breached is exactly why productivity improvement in HR and training functions has seemed so stalled.

Take my experience with a different health group. These were registered nurses—36,000 of them. The government where this group of nurses worked has a law that sets a lot of standards and requirements that aren't directly related to patient care, but which nurses need to know for their own legal protection. That's where their association was trying to help.

The standard way they did this was to hand their members the legislation and then administer an exam on its contents. The law was nearly three hundred pages of dry, tedious language. Comparable paper-based, open-book exams in other jurisdictions took about five hours out of their members' lives to complete.

You can imagine how much enthusiasm that generated.

Now, no offense to the folks who draft laws, but nurses are practical people. They've got more urgent stuff going on than wading through columns of legalese. So, how do we make that same material more engaging? More digestible? More meaningful? How do we connect what's in the text of the law to what a patient might say on the ward or a situation a nurse might face in the operating room?

How? We gamify. When the same legal material—every single word of it—was presented through a gamified experience, the nurses' association noticed a couple of exciting things. While the conventional test typically took four to five hours of their members' time, the gamified module covered the same ground in under two hours. And the feedback they got from their members was that it didn't even feel that long.

And another thing. Because properly gamified training can be accessed anywhere at any time, users can pick it up whenever *they* like, at their own pace and place. The payback is amazing. Although the nurses in this case were allowed two weeks to finish the legal module once they started, many of them completed it one.

The reason they were finishing early left the association just blown away. "These people are actually doing this stuff outside of their eight-hour workday now, which they don't have to, but they just are," they told us. Some nurses spent a few minutes with the module in the morning before work. Others got to work, then did a bit more.

So now, instead of a boring obligation that no one really wanted to buckle down to, they've got people learning the material on their time off—because it's *fun* to do so.

And they're doing it in less than half the time. That's what improving the productivity of training looks like.

A related objection I hear sometimes is that a gamified test or assessment module feels too easy, or that it doesn't feel enough like real work. That's actually almost the exact opposite of what's really the case. Testing that feels like work or seems hard can often give a false assessment of what a person knows.

It's a factor that many trainers are familiar with: learned helplessness. First isolated by psychologist Martin Seligman in the 1960s, this kind of helplessness arises from the anxiety that comes up for people who have had bad experiences with tests in the past. And it makes it almost impossible for them to access their real abilities when they feel under the gun of a written exam.

If it's a multiple-choice test at the end of a video, for example, they may fall back on the old, random, A-C-D-C-B-C-A-C-and-so-on approach. Or they may just lock up. Either way, what the test is telling the organization that is administering it isn't even close to a fair or accurate indication of what that person knows.

For too long this test-anxiety effect has just been accepted as an unavoidable noise factor in human resources assessment. It doesn't have to be.

When assessment elements are integrated into gamified learning, all that anxiety simply goes away. Because test moments happen within the "game" itself, the players often don't even realize they're being tested. This can make gamified assessment far more revealing than a conventional test. (In fact, this effect is so powerful that it can sometimes raise valid ethical questions, as we'll see.)

To recap: the resources behind the "game face" of gamified training can be just as deep and rigorous as anything on paper or in a PowerPoint, and more so than most of today's e-learning products. And the assessments they provide can be more penetrating than ever before. Users who thinks time is flying by because they're caught up in the experience of game "play" can reveal far more about their real understanding of critical content than they would sitting in a room sweating nervously under the watchful eye of a proctor. And they can do it in as little as half the time as they did before.

REASONS TO RESIST

So why is there still resistance among some managers and training specialists to gamification? A lot of it, I've found, arises from sources other than the actual strengths or weaknesses of this new alternative to long-standing practice.

Some of these sources of resistance are personal, even emotional. They may be a bit sensitive for training and HR professionals to confront. I know; I've been there. Early in my career, I sat on their side of the table as an instructional designer myself.

But at the same time, a lot of this emotional resistance is tied to some common misperceptions and—I'm sorry to have to say it—failures to think through the learner's reality fully. These are errors holding too many HR departments back from the productivity gains that gamification could unlock. We need to address both the misconceptions and the feelings.

And it's often not the professional trainer, the HR manager, or the organizational communicator who's at fault for failing to see the potential power of gamification for their missions. They may not even be entirely clear on what that mission really involves for their target audience.

I've truly been surprised by the number of organizations I've encountered in which the roles of trainer, subject expert, internal marketer, and human resources manager get confused. People with one skill set try to stretch it into areas they're not equipped for. They end up struggling to cope, bumping into other folks' functions, and generally suffering from confusion about their actual goals and tactics.

An individual might be tasked to conduct an internal marketing campaign, for example. It really entails training, but she doesn't realize that that's what she's doing. She's being asked to educate employees, but when it comes right down to it, she has no idea how to do that. She has never had to distill complex content down to the most relevant, task-critical items, let alone present it in the "byte-size" and just-in-time information packets that today's media-immersed employees expect. She may have even less idea how to isolate and devise training narratives for the critical decision moments that supercharge gamified learning.

I've encountered individuals who came to their role as organizational trainers—or whatever their actual title was—from professional and occupational backgrounds in education, psychology, and assessment on the organization's front lines, or from corporate culture and image management.

Sometimes these people know a lot about the content they want to get across, whether it's work-site safety or corporate mission statements or in-job requalifying. They're steeped in subject-matter expertise. But they have no expertise in training. They continue doing what has always been done before, because that looks like it must be the standard.

Even worse is when their own job performance is being assessed based on some crude metric, like how many learning modules they churn out each quarter. That's a surefire recipe for replicating the same-old, same-old as often as possible.

Sometimes it's the other way around. An individual comes from a training/HR background but has never walked the walk on the jobsite. He may be dropped into an assignment knowing plenty of theory-based tactics for conveying content—but with barely a clue about what content needs to be conveyed. When this happens, sometimes it's a lot easier for these people just to keep handing out the same binder their predecessor's predecessor did.

This can be dangerous, by the way. I mean physically dangerous. I worked with a client that delivered material to construction sites. Their operations relied on thousands of drivers maneuvering heavy trucks among cranes and earthmovers, and people in close quarters working on residential developments. The client's human resources department couldn't figure out why so many of these guys were getting injured on the job. After all, these workers were given safety "training."

What the company's well-educated trainers hadn't counted on however, was who their audience actually was. Most of their frontline coworkers operating the company's heavy equipment had low grade-school education, at best. Some were immigrants for whom English was a second language. The safety material the trainers handed out was too academic and complex for the audience. It was written at a level that might as well be Klingon to those guys.

The trainers could keep firing the same material to those workers over and over and over, and it still wouldn't get any traction.

But either way, whether trainers know the subject matter but not the training element, or the reverse, I feel for them. They're usually too busy keeping their heads above water on the unfamiliar side of their assignment to have the time to grasp all the advantages of gamification—far less to approach its next-level results with the old-fashioned techniques they're still working with.

Sometimes it's simply overload. I've encountered organizations where human resources, onboarding and in-service training, and performance assessment have been trimmed to the point where the HR professionals are run off their feet just delivering the material they inherited. Often, they don't have a spare moment to get their heads into the specific content of any single course or training element they're responsible for. And they certainly don't have time to imagine how they could begin to achieve their department's goals with more return to the organization, and more engagement for the employee, in less time.

The folks tasked with delivering the content are too pressed for time themselves to question the conventional formula that "more work equals more learning." They assume that quantity is quality, that the more time students spend on a subject, or the more material they've got to wade through while they're at it, the more learning happens. In my experience, there may be more teaching going on in that scenario, but there's often a lot less learning happening than the trainer imagines.

And, last on this list, there's basic human psychology. If you and your boss, and her boss before her, always did it this way, and it's always satisfied upper management before, then don't mess with something that's not broken, right?

Well, actually there are a couple of things not right about that.

For one thing, upper management may not be that satisfied after all. Not when human resources is the only division not booking gains in productivity like the ones observed in logistics, manufacturing, or sales.

Here's a real situation I came across. We had provided new training tools for a client and were waiting to see how they were rolled out and received. That's always an exciting and tense moment. But it didn't happen. Finally, after months of delays I called the executive vice president to ask him what was happening. He didn't know. He actually thought we'd dropped the ball.

He checked, and it turned out his lead trainer was refusing to release the gamified learning module. "She doesn't want to use the material because there's a bunch of people who are making six-figure salaries who will lose their jobs, even though they've been recycling the same curriculum year after year," the executive told me.

It turned out that the lead trainer was afraid that if she released the material we had developed, then her entire staff would be considered redundant. She figured that, instead of employees flying in from all over the continent to the head office for classroom instruction, people would receive the same training at their locations, on their desktops or handheld devices, and at their own pace.

It's natural not to want to lose your job. But this particular fear just shows, again, that some people haven't really understood what gamification entails. It's not dressing up the same old content with a burst of canned applause that goes off whenever you turn the page.

Gamification unleashes its potential only when it follows the careful design of a specific, situation-dependent learning trajectory hitched to the most powerful psychological and emotional drivers the global gaming industry has developed.

For training and HR professionals game for the challenge, this creates the opportunity for a whole lot *more* work than before, not less. Effectively gamifying legacy material calls for more focus, more discernment, and more creativity in these roles than ever before. In return, the practitioners using them achieve more: meeting goals sooner and with better outcomes. And gamification documents those increasingly valuable contributions to the organization's success in real time, building the case for professionals using them to earn greater recognition.

A GENERATIONAL IMPERATIVE

But there's another reason that even the very best examples of many old training and HR practices are broken in many organizations. It is that staying static is simply not an option for continued occupational relevance when your key audience is moving away from you.

The trucking company in my example performs a valuable role in society. But jobs that require only a valid commercial driver's license aren't the economy's growth sector. And wherever companies or organizations are competing for the most energetic, talented, and committed new recruits, they're confronting a generation with far different personal drivers than their Baby Boom elders.

I'm from the early cusp of the generations that have grown up as digital natives. I grew up with the original Nintendo Entertainment System (NES). My entire career has been spent dovetailing the extraordinary power of computer gaming with the nuts-and-bolts and sometimes bricks-and-mortar contexts of training objectives. The first company I started specialized in engaging school-age audiences with educational material. Some of those Millennial kids are your current employees or next wave of new recruits. I know how they think.

My generation and those coming up are not just digitally native—we're device agnostic. We've been raised with content delivered not just on-screen, but also flowing wirelessly to whatever device we happen to have in our hand—be that a tablet, a PC, or, almost universally, our smartphones. And we're mobile. We have no patience being tethered to one desk monitor, let alone being stuck in a room with a binder. Yet that's still what many organizations do when they're onboarding a new hire.

Trust me, I see it all the time it. And it doesn't work.

Some bright young Millennial hears a recruiter riff on how progressive and innovative their company is, how it's "leading-edge." Then on day one she's told to sit in front of a twenty-minute video of a guy giving a PowerPoint. She'll walk out. Literally, walk out.

Now HR is on the hook for the failed hire. So, the recruiter goes back to the training team and asks, "What the hell happened?" Then they'll ask the Millennial why she bailed, and that individual will say, "You guys lied. You're not a culturally or technologically progressive company at all."

Seriously, we're at a point in the generational change in new clients and employees where, if some human resources and training professionals don't adapt, they won't have a job.

An interesting thing though, and I'll come back to it, is this: when you serve up training in gamified form to different generations, what works well for the Millennial works equally well for the Boomer!

But sometimes it's not the organization's training professionals who stand in the way of seizing the gamification advantage. It could be the brand police.

I'm sorry. I have friends in marketing and branding who serve a valuable purpose. It is important to make sure an organization presents a consistent face and value proposition to its customers, its partners, and its own employees. But seriously, some brand guidelines verge on OCD.

I've found that the bigger the organization, the more likely they are to have a binder that dives into the tiniest details. It defines the fonts, the colors, and the images you're allowed to use to stay within brand guidelines. It may seem like a small thing, but those fonts may not even be Web-compatible. If that's the case, they may interfere with what users see in their experience of a gamified learning module.

But oddly enough the department most likely to resist gamification is the one you'd think would be soonest to seize on its power: the IT guys. And I get that. Hey, in a lot of ways, I'm an IT guy, too.

I get the way IT departments look at this stuff. It's that every time something new comes into their environment, it's a problem just by default. They're already busy enough dealing with emergencies—like the employee who panics when his computer doesn't work. IT asks, "Is it plugged in?" and it isn't.

Smartphones create an even bigger headache for IT. Now there's a wholesale shift to "BYOD"—where people are "bringing their own device" into work and demanding access to the network. The new nuisance IT complaint is, "My phone's not working." But it's a noncompany approved, off-brand device you bought on vacation in China.

Then along comes gamification. And the IT guys just see something else new that they have to learn about, deal with, and rescue their tech-clueless coworkers from.

And sure, IT staff may also share a bit of the same fear the HR manager had whenever a company brings in a third-party service: "Oh my God, am I going to be pushed out of a job because this service is doing *my* job?"

But there's an even deeper level to IT department resistance to gamification. It's a control thing.

That's not necessarily wrong. It comes from trying to protect the organization's data and digital assets from the bad guys out there. That leads many of the field's professionals to default to a bunker mentality. They want to keep their organization and fellow employees safe inside their network and its firewall.

But for gamification to unleash its full power, it has to live outside the walls.

The reason nurses are working on their mandated legal knowledge on the bus to work, or in the café on a break, is because *they can*. In that way, gamified learning is just like the latest viral MMOG (massively multiplayer online game). It's always ready when the users are, at their place and pace, anywhere they're within reach of the cloud. On any device. With any screen size or operating system.

And all of that, for the most part, has to take place outside IT's network walls. IT guys tend to find that very, very uncomfortable.

The good news, of course, is that cloud security has advanced at Internet speed. Web-based platforms are now good enough for activities like online financial transactions. They can keep an organization's data and personnel information just as safe outside its network firewall as inside.

The payback when gamified learning is released from the workplace is that it becomes part of the learner's wider life and routine. They're bringing it into their homes and downtimes because it feels as if it's designed for them. (Of course it is!) They're participating outside of work hours because it doesn't feel like work.

This chapter has mostly been about some of the misunderstandings surrounding gamified learning. In the next, we'll meet the real thing and begin to see why it really is so exciting.

But the gang in IT can relax.

CHAPTER 3

GAMIFYING WITH INTENT

———

Gaming. Video gaming. Computer gaming. Platform games. Online games and off-line games. Games on your PC, games on your phone. Single-player games and massively multiplayer games.

With so much variety in the world of digital entertainment gaming, it's no wonder people get confused about what gamification in business and organizational training is.

And because pretty much everyone by now has played a digital game of one kind or another, whether it was Tetris or Super Mario Bros. or Fallout 4, everyone has a personal idea of what gaming is about. That usually just further confuses things.

Because gamification isn't a game at all.

Rock-paper-scissors is a game. Monopoly is a game. Pokémon Go and the Olympics and the Super Bowl are games. Part of the appeal is that no one knows in advance specifically how they'll turn out. In fact, unpredictability is part of their appeal.

Gamification uses insights, devices, and techniques that come from the world of games. Gamified learning can be fun. But it's not a game. Every move has been closely planned in advance to follow a certain trajectory and bring the "player" to a certain outcome.

Games engage our interest and emotions. They often have a narrative story. Will Mario rescue the princess? Will you and your Minecraft constructions survive the Creepers? But as long as you're having fun and playing through, the folks who created the game and its rules really don't care if you come out afterward at all changed from how you went in. They're not interested in whether you know anything more. They couldn't care less if you have acquired new skills that will help you better handle a workplace situation.

The better way to think about gamification is not as part of the gaming world at all, but as part of the much bigger and more important universe of training and education. Those activities were estimated to be a $49 *trillion*-dollar industry worldwide in 2015. That's about 490 times the size of the digital gaming industry, by the way, but who's counting?

So yes, bringing the arcade to the office means adopting psychology and technology from the world of Final Fantasy or Grand Theft Auto. It takes other ideas, such as task trajectory and rewards for activity, from there, too. But it does so in the corporate space in service to the serious organizational goals of education, awareness, and assessment.

Gamified content wants you to be just as immersed in its activities as you might be in getting your SimCity to flourish. But by the time you are finished having fun, it also wants you to know more, acquire an important new skill, or demonstrate some real-world competence. It's built to "play." But there is always a serious intent and motivation behind the play action.

Another important difference: the people who invent games usually aren't concerned with how well or poorly you personally do at them. They may keep track of your play, not just to give you a score—like points on a pinball machine—but because they want to know which parts of their game hold your attention the best. Those are features they'll develop in future games. They also track play for opportunities to offer in-game purchases.

But as for what players have "learned" in the game, they don't really track that.

Instructors, however, care a lot about what their employees or other learners are picking up. They want to know as much as they can about it. Gamified learning modules watch their players' every move to reveal the answer in detail.

THE ZOMBIE APOCALYPSE

When the Pentagon unleashed a zombie apocalypse on US military planners, as they did in 2011, it was no game. It reflected a deadly serious preoccupation for the Pentagon: the ability to mobilize its vast resources to respond to multiple threats from several unexpected directions at once.

The designers of the training exercise known as CONPLAN 8888 had a very specific problem: how to test military planners' ability to perform in the face of a disorienting cascade of unexpected security threats. The intent was to identify specific weak points in the ability of the different armed services to cooperate and coordinate their responses.

The solution accommodated both goals. The Pentagon dreamed up an imaginary scenario in which eight different kinds of "zombies"—from heavily armed ones, to radioactive ones, to vegetarian zombies that destroyed crops—"attacked" essential domestic assets like food and water supplies, all at once. Senior commanders monitoring the exercise watched Air Force, Navy, Marine, and Army planners deploy a range of military assets in reply. (The zombies were beaten back, by the way, and America survived to fight another day.)

The Pentagon's imaginary zombie apocalypse generated an insane amount of pickup and enthusiasm. "If you suspend reality for a few minutes," supervising officers wrote in their after-action report, "this type of training scenario can actually take a very dry, monotonous topic and turn it into something rather enjoyable."

The colorfully conceived zombies were far less important than the information the game revealed to senior commanders about how their men and women in uniform stepped up as the "invasion" stress-tested their response protocols.

Two features qualified the US military's "zombie attack" as more than just a game. One was its deadly serious purpose of helping ensure that the country's defense system was, literally, ready for anything. The other was how the narrative scenario revealed players' responses during a less guarded, more authentic engagement with the problem.

The zombie apocalypse was way out-of-the-box thinking for a pretty conservative organization like the military. But while it may have been a type of war game, it wasn't yet full-on gamification.

Let me explain.

For all the inventiveness that went into its concept, CON-PLAN 8888 was actually run out of paper binders, with observers physically present at the players' locations. It wasn't digitized or delivered across mobile platforms.

There may have been security or other reasons for that, but as we'll see in detail later on, the analog (nondigital) paper platform the Pentagon employed deprived it of an enormous amount of potential real-time monitoring feedback, which can only be gathered effectively when training is fully gamified—that is to say, when the training game goes digital.

I have been developing gamified training for more than a decade. That's longer than it has been identified in the human resources space as a mode of training. In that time, my clients have used it for an astonishingly large variety of purposes. One uses it to onboard union members into financial literacy. Another helps senior executives understand the finer nuances of pension education. A third employed gamification, and a 1940s murder-mystery theme, to get university students excited about accounting.

What they all had in common was a critical training or awareness component. There was some skill or insight that the organization wanted to persist in the "player" after he or she came to the end of an awareness module. Usually administrators were also keen to *know exactly* how much of that knowledge seemed to have stuck with the learner by the time he or she put the module down.

At my company, we have made that mission ours. We have taken inspiration from games like L.A. Noire and Plants vs. Zombies to gamify how users reach awareness goals. We made the experience more engaging, the assessment tools more seamless and unobtrusive, and the time more productive for both learner and trainer or HR professional.

If the experience of being onboarded into your organization, for example, feels as if it was designed with a new hire's specific learning style, she is more likely to embrace it. It doesn't feel like work, so she's more likely to do some of her mandatory preparation on her own time. In fact, she's already buying in emotionally to your corporate vision.

So, games are for fun. Gamification, by contrast, always carries a serious intent. This may be to leave someone with a new awareness or capability or to help organizations get better insights into their members or employees. It's usually some of both.

SCALE AND INTIMACY

But in the contemporary, always-connected work/life space, where "BYOD" rules, that's not enough. After a decade of experimentation, I have found that three further features have to be present to truly unlock the power of gamified training and assessment:

- 👾 It is digitally distributed to many "players."
- 👾 It is device agnostic.
- 👾 It resides in the cloud.

These qualities reveal why the genesis of high-impact gamification had to await the massive uptake of digitization and personal digital devices.

I suppose you could develop a board-and-token-type game with the feel of Monopoly or Clue that used some of those games' features to interest players in a more serious subject and leave them with new knowledge. Trivial Pursuit does something like that, by happy accident, for half a dozen players at a time.

But without open-ended scalability, device agnosticism, and cloud delivery, gamification on a board makes as much sense in the twenty-first century as communicating with a branch office by letter or hiring a town crier for your new promotion.

Digital distribution to many players matters for two reasons. One is the obvious economic one of scale and return on investment. Very few organizations can afford to create a new and unique training experience for every individual employee entering or in service.

But the second reason to want unlimited scalability to multiple players is more important. Only such a *population* of players provides the database to leverage gamification's most powerful assessment insights.

Each "play" of a game module can tell administrators more about the individual playing than even the most invasively proctored paper-and-pen exam. But my clients almost always find that their most revealing insights come from being able to examine the aggregate and comparative information that flows from the real-time monitoring and archiving of each play event. It's the data resource that supports the analytic strength of deep scoring, which I'll delve into in chapter 6. And it's one of the most powerful reasons I know of for organizations to gamify their training and awareness approach.

Device agnosticism goes against the grain for some IT departments. We talked earlier about how some tech staff don't want to let any of their fellow employees outside the protective firewall of their corporate network. That just doesn't work in the twenty-first century.

Take a look around the café. The bus. The airport boarding lounge. What's everyone doing? They're checking their smartphones. It doesn't matter whether they're in a three-piece suit and tie, a hoodie and kicks, or a gran'ma bun with a bag of knitting. Smartphone penetration is so close to universal in developed—and develop*ing*—countries that the difference isn't worth worrying about.

It's old news that this has blurred the boundary between work and private time. There are arguments about whether that's a good thing or not. I'm just going to accept that it's a *real* thing. It's the way our society is going, and forward-leaning organizations are going to respond to the reality of smart-device ubiquity and act accordingly.

The smartphone, or the personal tablet or computer, is *the* way most people engage with the world beyond their kitchen table these days. Not only is it foolish and limiting to ignore that fact, but ignoring it also forecloses several key opportunities for training effectiveness and HR insight.

One is intimacy. We love our smartphones. We really do. How many of us take ours to bed with us for a last peek at our e-mail before we lay it on the bedside table? How many of us panic when we think we've lost it? The smartphone is the 24/7 valet, maid, and personal companion of the twenty-first century.

As such, the smartphone offers whatever resides on it a privileged platform of intimacy with the user. That's why app-makers covet a place on your phone screen! When you make gamified training content available for learners to pursue in that same intimate space, you really begin to leverage what it can do.

This intimacy helps break down the mental walls erected around the work site and the time clock. It lures players into learning on the bus or the back porch. Maybe I'm on my way to work and have a twenty-minute commute. In that time, I could earn ten game badge rewards. By the time I'm settling at my desk with my coffee, I just completed a training module.

When we shift the user's relationship to training from one of "work" to one of eager engagement, we also lower the anxiety and learned helplessness that unavoidably distort conventional test scores. When testing is integrated seamlessly into the gamified play experience within that willing relationship, it's much more likely to produce accurate, honest reflections of knowledge and performance.

But to secure that intimacy and invitation into users' off-work life, gamified learning must be available at their own pace and in their own place. It needs to be there on whatever device that users employ, wherever they are in reach of the Web. Which leads me directly to the last criterion for real, fully functional gamification.

Gamification resides in the cloud. This is partly a rather obvious implication of the previous point. To reach users where they live and go about their day, at their pace and place, your gamified learning module can't be locked up in the network vault. It can't only be available at a terminal in a training center. It has to be a click away in the café. So it has to live in the cloud.

For the IT guys, however, this should really be viewed as a good thing—not an added threat. The evolution of cloud computing has made available numerous off-the-shelf tools for building cloud-based elements and scripting their events. That lowers costs compared to developing customized software specifically to work on an enterprise network.

Among those tools are numerous choices of application programming interfaces (APIs). These programs plug cleanly and securely into existing enterprise data software. They can transfer data from people playing their gamified training modules at work or home, back across network firewalls, and deposit them in any digital containers that administrators choose. And they can do it in real time, without inviting security concerns and affordably.

Hence the definition I give at the front of this book:

> *Real* gamification uses "design and insights from video games in the organizational space to engage trainees on multiple devices as they follow a learning narrative to targeted outcomes, generating real-time assessment data."

NOT GAMIFICATION

There are also some things gamification is *not*. Don't confuse it with frankly more primitive digital tools such as e-learning platforms, nor with vastly more sophisticated ones such as immersive simulators. Doing that has misled some HR and training professionals into thinking they know what gamification is—and dismissing it as nothing new. Or perhaps as way out of their league budget-wise. They're losing out on its benefits.

Gamification is not e-learning. Too often I meet companies that have enormous e-learning modules. When I take a look, I find that they have just vacuumed up all their old content from some binder library, turned it into a desktop file, and made users "click here to continue" instead of turning the page. Or they've put a PowerPoint online for people to flip through and thrown in a few screens of questions at the end.

That's not gamification. It's simply making people go through the same material on a screen that they used to leaf through in a package of documents. As a client of mine likes to put it, that's "e-boring."

Nor do e-learning platforms such as Adobe Captivate and Articulate Storyline equal gamification. That class of product has a place. It provides a framework for sequencing and presenting e-learning elements. More recent updates have tacked on the capability of allowing users to earn points or collect badges as they go.

But simply adding a prize for using the platform doesn't gamify e-learning. I've often heard points and badges described as "the toy in the Cracker Jacks"—something you get just by opening the box and eating enough popcorn. They're decoration on the content, rather than functional. They can't produce any useful insight for an administrator looking over a learner's shoulder. That's faux gamification.

E-learning *platforms* are also no more than that: they're bare foundations for content creation, not creative services. And just like a PowerPoint presentation, they are only as good as the person or team that uses them. Simply buying a technology platform isn't all it takes to create learning material that seizes a user's attention, any more than being able to afford a private airplane makes you an airline pilot. Successfully using e-learning platforms depends on the design skills of people whose expertise may be strong in human resources or subject matter, but not so much in narrative and visual design.

Two final shortcomings of e-learning platforms are these. The first is they are designed to present content in a linear progression, which doesn't easily allow users to learn the way most people do naturally, following their interests, making choices, branching off from and coming back to the main theme. The second is that e-learning platforms cannot follow a learner's play and present challenges tailored to their stage of progress.

And so far, the e-learning platforms I have examined lack a user-friendly ability to publish their content easily to the Web for access via the cloud. They fail that critical test of truly gamified learning delivery.

Gamification entails a variety of specialized human skills that are generally more economically sourced from a service provider. (Before the end of the book, I'll talk about how to assess the qualification of a provider.) That's certainly going to be more expensive than a Captivate or Storyline licence.

But it's also far, far less expensive than another training technology that gamification sometimes gets confused with: simulation, of the kind a jet cockpit simulator provides for flight training.

That kind of immersive environment is designed to replicate the experience of reality as closely as possible. It allows an operator to throw the user virtually into a wide variety of physically challenging situations safely. It features microsecond-by-microsecond monitoring of the flight crew's actions, archived for replay and later assessment.

Such a simulator can also cost in the realm of $3 to over $130 million. It can only be used by one player at a time—either an individual pilot or a flight crew playing as a team. It represents an enormous investment for a very specific purpose. And it may not be suitable for the other training content that an organization needs to convey.

While gamification design uses a great deal of realism in its elements, it doesn't try to duplicate reality at the minute level of detail that a flight simulator does.

Instead, gamification leverages players' imaginations to engage emotional involvement in the same way that the printed text of a Harry Potter novel does. OK, it generally uses more pictures, fewer words, and a few things that move across the screen and go "zing!" But it doesn't try to duplicate the physical sensation of flying around the turrets at Hogwarts School of Witchcraft and Wizardry as simulation would.

Good gamification undeniably costs more than throwing an old PowerPoint presentation up on a video screen. It's more involved, as well as more expensive, than buying a Captivate or Storyline licence and expecting it to solve the training-productivity block.

In return, however, gamification engages users and provides assessment data at stunning new levels of intensity that are far closer to what those full-meal flight physical simulators generate than any earlier training approach, at a price that's much closer to earth.

I'll examine the many ways that real gamification brings new value to training and the human resources function in a company or organization next, in chapter 4.

CHAPTER 4

ADDICTIVE LEARNING

———

Now that we're clear what gamification is and isn't, we still want to know: Why is it such a big deal? And why is it worth the extra cost compared to an off-the-shelf e-learning platform? In one word: return.

The application of insights from entertainment gaming to learning objectives is a breakthrough moment for knowledge transfer and assessment. That makes it a breakthrough for human resources and training professionals as well. It constitutes an altogether new and amazingly powerful level of features in the previously fixed hierarchy of training technologies and cost options.

Once upon a time the classroom whiteboard—or, in the really olden days, the *black*board—was state-of-the-art in knowledge transfer. Think of that as the bottom of the training-tech hierarchy.

For many organizations, it's still the tried-and-true fallback. But it comes with all the snooze-inducing associations of school. It depends on stressful in-classroom testing for assessments. And in this age of distributed staff and partner networks, it can quickly get expensive to fly people in from distant locations and accommodate them in hotels in order to put them though in-classroom training and testing.

The 1960s brought the overhead projector: the bright light, dark room, and flustered presenter getting all those transparencies confused.

But the next widely adopted innovation in knowledge presentation didn't really show up until 1990. May of that year was when Microsoft first released PowerPoint. It dressed and cleaned up the content that used to be scrawled with a marker—or chalk!—on the board or transparency. It accommodated tidy tables and photographs or other images. It could run on its own and even animate its slide transitions with sound effects. The results could be reused and shared easily and endlessly. When the

Internet came along, presentations could just as easily be recorded and put up on Vimeo or YouTube.

Presentation software is now as ubiquitous as the whiteboard. Probably more so. You used to have to buy a program like Microsoft Office or Apple's Keynote to get presentation software. These days, the basic capabilities come preloaded on most enterprise and personal computers, and Google Docs offers a version for free.

But anyone who has sat through a bad PowerPoint presentation knows that the platform alone doesn't produce a gripping presentation. Unreadable graphs or slides full of text don't get the point across. They just put the audience to sleep—or drive it out of the room.

Products like Adobe Captivate and Articulate Storyline are presentation software on steroids—with a bit more power, but similar limitations. They add interactive capabilities that allow users to take quizzes and tests. But without significant additional customizing, those products don't go much further than PowerPoint. They're hard to deliver over the Internet or to distant personal computers, tablets, or smartphones.

Unlike presentation software, these platforms don't come free. They require group or individual licensing payments.

And because they are still only tools and not services, their successful implementation depends on the proficiency of the individual or team using them—just like PowerPoint.

If, like many trainers, you're a subject-matter expert in a given area, now you also have to know all the tricks and nuances of delivering that content in a technology brand new to you. That's a very unreasonable management ask. And it's where I've seen a lot of organizations get into trouble.

A technology company will sell trainers on something, and they'll think, "Yeah, I got this. I can do it my own." But when it comes right down to it, they don't know where to start or even what questions to ask. The project falls off schedule. Suddenly an option that looked cost-effective at the outset is becoming quite pricey and producing disappointing results.

Until now, the next jump in training technology and cost was a big one: from the video of your PowerPoint up to the full-on training simulator.

First developed to train astronauts and then military and commercial pilots, training simulators are now available for a variety of activities, such as driving a semitrailer or working on an oil derrick. The Xbox and PlayStation host any number of simulator games, from aviation to NASCAR racing, available for just a few bucks.

The real thing, complete with an immersive capsule that can be made to shake and rattle like an airplane in distress, starts at seven figures and could potentially go over nine. A fully dressed commercial jet simulator will set you back more than $150 million, for example. That means that even the relatively few organizations that can afford real simulators at all will likely want to reserve full-feature simulation for only the highest-stakes training contexts.

THE POWER OF SIMULATION WITHOUT THE PRICE

Gamification brings a new option to this limited hierarchy of training technology and costs. It's much more than a mere platform. It's more like a multifaceted discipline.

To get gamification right requires a specific blend of skills—instructional and digital designers, graphic artists, storytellers, and programmers. And each contributor has to be at the top of his or her game. The final user experience and organization return will only be as good as the least talented member of the creative team.

For all but the very biggest organizations, it will generally make much more sense to bring a specialized gamification partner into a project than to make the significant investment to develop in-house expertise. That would likely be true even to manage a complete program of gamifying legacy content. (I'll discuss what to look for in providers in chapter 7.)

In contrast to e-learning platforms, which are available for license fees in the four-figure range, competent gamification more typically starts in the mid-five figures. The payback for the extra investment comes in the supercharged training effectiveness and assessment data it provides. Both e-learning and gamification bear comparison to the effectiveness and data from full-meal occupational simulations—but at a tiny fraction of their cost.

Now, sure, there is a big difference between gamified learning and fully immersive simulation. Gamification doesn't try to put you *right there*, feeling the slither as your simulated semitrailer skids off an icy highway. That alone accounts for a whole lot of savings. Immersive physical alternative realities don't come cheap!

But leveraging the unequalled power of the human imagination, gamification nonetheless brings a surprising amount of the simulator's most important capabilities within reach of everyday organizations. For that matter, even an organization that can afford a simulator could save money by gamifying its candidate assessments, screening out people who are poor risks for the larger investment that simulator training time represents.

What are the critical capabilities that gamification shares with much more powerful and expensive immersive simulation? There are three. One is player engagement. A second is scenario running. And the third is the wealth of real-time tracking data generated for later assessment. These are all important.

In a simulator, the sensation of physical immersion in a replicated emergency can bring sweat out on a veteran pilot's forehead and leave him shaking afterward. But in fact, the history of entertainment shows that you don't need all that technology to get your pulse moving and mind racing.

An inviting scenario, a hook for the imagination to run with, and a task at which the player can win or lose are the essentials of both compelling games and compelling storytelling. They can turn even a highly abstract screen game such as Tetris into an emotional roller coaster. Gamification leverages this built-in desire to put ourselves "in the game" to get learners to put themselves "into the subject" with the same emotional commitment.

Engaged learners absorb material faster and more completely than disengaged ones. That is a simple and well-established fact known to every parent supervising her kid's homework. In an organizational training context, however, the players' willing emotional and mental investment in the fiction of the game narrative does something more. It disarms their defensiveness and distrust. Minds become more receptive to new information. Responses become more natural and authentic.

Like simulator-based training, gamification doesn't leave events to the player. It can throw users into challenges designed either to advance their skills or to test them, in a variety of ways limited only by the imagination. (Even with zombies!)

One of my company's most successful projects did that for construction-service truck drivers. The visual on-screen scene portrayed a typical work site with features that a driver might encounter there: dumpsters and portable construction toilets, pedestrian passersby, and heavy equipment. Among these were several features that could pose problems or injury: inadequate fencing and a temporary toilet that unauthorized personnel could use, inviting liability issues.

Drivers put into the scene in their gamified safety training were far more likely to spot and avoid actual safety hazards later, on real job sites, than drivers who had received only text-based instruction.

And just like a $100 million simulator, gamified training tracks an individual's "play" each step of the way. How long do users spend with a particular challenge? How often do they "check the manual" by looking at resource material? What time of day do they "play"? Or where in the gamified module do they drop out entirely?

Meanwhile, users' enhanced presence in the learning moment during a module's assessment phases gives a more accurate representation of what they have really learned. I'll dig deeper into the many potential returns from gamification's data-tracking capabilities in chapter 6.

My point here is that these results are what make gamification the breakthrough it is for productivity in the training and resource space. Gamification makes these learning and assessment capabilities available in a price range that's a tiny fraction of the only other technology capable of delivering similar returns.

GETTING TO "KNOW"

Productivity in training and HR has always been a little hard to demonstrate. In default, many practitioners make the simple equation with time. The longer someone studies, the more they have learned. A related idea is the "no pain, no gain" theory. The idea that the harder the content is on your head—and the slower time seems to go as you're plowing through it—the more you'll absorb.

Strangely, a lot of HR professionals and senior executives also tend to think that increasing productivity is just a matter of math. It means squeezing more people through the same old training more quickly. "We don't want to pay them any longer than necessary to learn this stuff, so the faster we can get through this, the better." Or it means packing more learners in front of a lecturer at a time—the same idea behind college freshmen classes with hundreds of students.

These notions are not just contradictory. They should really be irrelevant. If more time equals better learning, why try to squeeze as many people as possible through an hour's instruction? Yet one of the major focal points for every client we have is: How long will it take the learner to complete the module?

Here's the thing: efficiency and productivity are about *getting something done*, about *producing* some intended result. Productivity on the manufacturing line doesn't just mean moving parts along as fast as possible. It also means that each stage in the process is done right. It doesn't help if a fabric-cutter is turning out twice as many glove blanks as his coworker, if they all have three fingers!

The "product" in training and human resources assessment isn't as clear as it is on the manufacturing line, but it's no mystery either. It's all about knowledge exchange. Half of the exchange going on is the awareness that is successfully conveyed to a trainee. The other half is the knowledge that HR administrators can extract about those being trained.

Productivity in the corporate HR space is how much of both those transfers can be accomplished for a given investment in time and resources. In short: time is part of the productivity picture, but not all of it.

Time can be misspent, for one thing. I know an oil company, one of the largest in the country, that hired a group of graduates after two, three, even four years in postsecondary technical programs. Out on the job site on day one, they were complete train wrecks. "They had perfect grades and commendations from instructors," the company told me. "But everything they know in theory doesn't apply in practice."

The flip side of that failure is overloading trainees with everything in the manual and background binder when there are really only a few critical points or processes they need to know.

Today's Millennials and those coming up behind them are used to picking up information on an as-needed basis. They'll go to YouTube for the video briefing on fixing a toilet when they happen to need that knowledge—not before.

Gamification suits that learning style. It provides optional background help as users call for it and to the extent that they need it. It doesn't waste their time, or the organization's, forcing them to pay attention to noncritical material that's not relevant to the task at hand.

Other skills are so important that the time it takes to convey them should really be considered irrelevant, or at least very secondary, to their mastery. Within limits, should a trade accreditation agency really care how long it takes a welder to learn how to light his oxyacetylene torch safely?

"TEACHING" ISN'T "LEARNING"

The reality is that "teaching" time doesn't equal "learning" time.

The Chipotle restaurant chain suffered a painful consumer scandal when its customers began getting sick. The cause was unsanitary food handling. All the chain's employees had passed a nationally mandated safe food-handling exam. But clearly something was missing in their training. When employees were asked about the exam they'd taken, they said revealing things like, "I have no clue how that test relates to me making a burrito."

That is not to say that time never counts. A related challenge for HR managers is making sure new hires take the time to learn their new employer's corporate mission and values—or even their own nonwage benefits. To someone who's focused on starting a new job, those can seem like pretty low priorities.

One of my company's first projects was an "onboarding game"—that's really what they called it—for a big electrical utility that wanted new hires to be made aware of its service-oriented culture. The company sent each new hire one e-mail with our gamified readiness module and the invitation to click "to get ready for your first day on the job."

I had actually told the client not to expect more than one in every four or five hires to take the initiative to click through and play the full game. After all, they weren't being paid yet. In fact, 80 percent of them finished the module *before* they went on the payroll clock. Now that's higher productivity!

Allowing people to advance through subject-matter content at their own pace and in their own place reduces several of the unnecessary pressures normally associated with time-marked activities. If you know you only have the duration of a classroom or video lesson to complete a learning module, you're bound to be more nervous about getting it done in time. If you can go at your own speed, checking resource material at a click when you need to, you'll naturally feel more comfortable. People who know the subject well will speed through it. Others can take the time they need to get up to speed on the content, revisit resources, or retry challenges as many times as it takes to confirm their understanding.

Of course, how are you going to get a learner to do something over again several times until he or she gets it, if the experience sucks? That's another place where the emotional magic of gamification comes in. Think of a successful game like Super Mario, and how many times most players fail at the first try whenever Mario has to learn a new move. Yet they keep at it, and eventually they get it.

That's what you want for your trainees, right? Such strong enthusiasm for the material that they'll keep coming back to it, even when they're *not* getting it yet.

In other respects, time can be both flexible and a strong indicator of how much a learner is absorbing. In a written paper exam, it's impossible for a marker to tell from a completed test who finished the test in record time, and who struggled and hesitated at each question.

With gamified training, that same administrator can track a user's activity time at every stage of the module. Some players may click through parts of a learning module in no time, because they already have the knowledge at the tips of their fingers. Others may just be taking random stabs at a step before they move on without learning a thing.

At this level of monitoring detail, letting a few best-in-class practitioners of whatever skill is being covered play the gamified module can create a benchmark profile of someone who's "got it." Comparing trainees' play to the profile can then help distinguish those who really do get it from those who are just skipping through the activity without a clue.

Gamification done right—that is to say, delivered through the cloud to personal digital devices—enhances organizational productivity in technical ways, too. The productivity formula isn't a matter of time cost just for learners but also for organizations.

Companies whose IT departments insist on keeping every contact with their employees tightly controlled inside their networks sacrifice a significant benefit: those employees could be accessing corporate training on their own time. Organizations that decide, perhaps for branding reasons, that they absolutely must control their own mobile application on every possible smartphone, screen, or desktop quickly find that's not sustainable.

The problem is that there are too many different iterations of smart-device operating systems out there. No IT department can keep up. The effort isn't worth it unless having an OS-native app working on every single conceivable device is somehow utterly mission-critical to their company. But then the IT department wouldn't have time to work on much else.

Android-based devices in particular are subject to a problem that developers call fragmentation. And it is a nightmare. There are more than 5,000 Android devices on the market. If you try to build a learning module to work on all the Android devices, then you'll spend the rest of your life monitoring them and fixing things.

Good gamification lives on the Web for that reason. Every device has a Web browser by default, and Internet connectivity is getting more universal all the time. That doesn't do away with all the possible game-play or display issues. Each of the half dozen or so browsers in wide use has its peculiarities. Desktop screens are huge compared to phones. But that's still better than more than 5,000 smartphone varieties to plan for! And usually the most burdensome technical chore this requires of learners is to update their browsers to a more recent version.

So, I urge anyone thinking about gamifying training material for the first time to abandon the idea that simply putting through "more widgets per hour" enhances employee productivity.

In the training and human resources space, productivity is the outcome of several squishy factors, but the bottom line is pretty clear. Forget about how much teaching happened. What matters is how much learning happened? And how do you know?

Gamification produces more learning, and more insight about what learning has happened, than any previous training technology with a price tag below many millions of dollars. And while time shouldn't be the be-all and end-all of productivity criteria, gamification also usually accomplishes those goals in less employer-paid trainee time than any other approach—including those big-ticket simulators.

Classroom teaching, presentation software, and the same content delivered on e-learning platforms rely on a learner's personal discipline to buckle down to the subject. They almost invite the student to consider it work to learn. Immersive simulators use expensive technology to capture a learner's willing engagement.

Gamification uses psychology. I'll talk more about how gamifiers do that in chapter 5.

"THE GREATEST FORM OF HUMAN HAPPINESS"

Here I want to talk about the huge wins when human resources and training practitioners can stop wasting so much time and effort fighting their students' natural instinct to boredom.

When those employees or other clients are recast as active and engaged players instead of dull students, the whole dynamic alters. Instead of working overtime to keep reluctant interest alive, content and training specialists get to—and have to—focus on only the most pivotal, relevant knowledge that must get across. And they can do it, confident that the game narrative will keep the players' interest level high.

Achieving this engagement is the secret sauce of gamified training. But in fact, there are no secrets. The best entertainment game and Web designers have this all figured out—right down to the basic psychology.

Game designer Jane McGonigal is also an educational theorist. She has an explanation for how this works in her book *Reality Is Broken: Why Games Make Us Better and How They Can Change the World*. It describes the feelings we get when we're immersed in a game.

Games are "highly structured, self-motivated hard work," she writes, "an opportunity to focus our energy, with relentless optimism, at something we're good at (or getting better at) and enjoy." During them, "we regularly achieve the greatest form of happiness available to human beings: intense, optimistic engagement with the world around us."

Wow. Consider the power of that statement. Instead of associating learning with work, with a hard slog through unfamiliar territory, with stumbles and mistakes and possible failure when the inevitable exam comes due, game play associates learning with the best sort of positive feelings any of us can experience.

That doesn't happen by accident. Entertainment games are consciously designed to achieve two psychologically critical effects: heightened expectation and then a dopamine burst to the brain as the player takes some action that delivers the sense of a win.

In a first-person-shooter type game, there are those moments of suspense when your avatar walks into the labyrinth of play. There's the adrenaline burst when the anticipated enemy unexpectedly appears. Then the dopamine rush comes when he explodes in a burst of your gunfire.

Whatever you think of any social messages embedded in that particular sequence of screen actions, it is minutely staged to seize the player's attention. As the *Washington Post* wrote recently about the powerful, even disturbing, hold that some video entertainment games can have on adolescent minds: "These games are deliberately designed, with the help of psychology consultants, to make players want to keep playing, and they are available on every platform—gaming consoles, computers, smartphones."

Some of these techniques are subtler than the dopamine rush of blowing up an imaginary enemy. There's the frustration factor, for example. If you can make a task just difficult enough before a successful response triggers a reward, the player will be *more* motivated to stay with it than if she wins right away every time.

Do you have a Facebook app on your smartphone? Have you ever noticed that little processing bar that slides from left to right as your page is loading? They don't need that. They could bring the page up in a fraction of a second. They delay it, and give you that bar, on purpose. They know that the delay enhances your anticipation for seeing your news feed—and will jolt up your dopamine hit when the page finally loads.

It's a little like those dinner hosts who make you wait to sit down at the table so you'll be good and hungry when the meal finally arrives!

I learned that from another of my idea heroes: Nir Eyal, the author of *Hooked: How to Build Habit-Forming Products*.

There are many of these techniques, and they work. The *Post*'s writer was concerned about the "steep rise in the number of parents worried that their kids are in fact addicted, or at least compulsively devoted, to [computer] games."

And perhaps rightly so. Eyal explained his ideas at a conference I attended to accept an award for one of our projects. He warned us in the audience to "be careful. If you use the principles in my book, you may be creating the next smoking habit."

But he also said this: "If you're in the audience and you're building online or digital education, you should be trying as hard as you can to get everyone addicted."

As much as "addiction" to video games may be an emerging threat for some, the term captures the powerful attraction that effective game design has had on millions of men and women who have spent countless hours immersed by their PlayStation, Xbox, Nintendo, or even a multi-player computer game. Gamification brings that same power to captivate and enthrall your employees' attention into the office for the benefit of training and awareness.

But it takes the coordinated talents of a range of conceptual, creative, design, and execution specialists to produce a compelling entertainment video game, one that creates an immersive on-screen experience for the user. The same is true when creating successful gamification.

In the next two chapters, I'll look more closely at the process of creating materials that trigger "addictive" learning. In chapter 5, I'll discuss how putting the user experience in the foreground can better achieve the instructor's goals. Then in chapter 6, I'll show you how embedding assessment in the experience of game play can unlock a wealth of new feedback data.

CHAPTER 5

THE LEARNING TRAJECTORY

———

We're all on a path. Only the mindful are on a trajectory. Those are the people with a specific destination and plan for getting there.

Too much of old-fashioned teaching simply throws a lot of material in front of students and leaves them largely to find their own way. That's like taking a child to the edge of the forest and saying, "In you go." Then you're surprised when he gets lost and never comes back out!

Gamification begins with a trajectory: a plan tightly tailored to the material that needs to be conveyed, the people who need to know it, and the setting where it will matter. Just as military targeting specialists plot the course that a cruise missile is going to take, every stage and waypoint of the learning game trajectory is planned.

Of course, our target is a lot more benign. We just want to improve employees' performance and assessment as it relates to the realities of their occupation and workplace setting. For that, we need to ensure that players who set out on a training module complete it and demonstrate that they have actually acquired the knowledge or awareness required.

Organizational and training experts Jim Williams and Steve Rosenbaum identified what they called a Learning Pathway more than a decade ago. They described it as "the ideal sequence of learning activities that drives employees to reach proficiency in their job in the shortest possible time." They told trainers to look at learning as a holistic process, rather than a one-time day or week in the classroom. Advanced trainers and skilled HR professionals who applied this thinking found they could reduce wasted input and bring people to proficiency more consistently in as little as half the time required by conventional methods.

Gamification puts the rocket fuel in Williams and Rosenbaum's theory. It gives trainers new tools to ignite learners'—players'!—interest and keep them motivated and engaged at every stage of their journeys. And, going beyond Williams and Rosenbaum entirely, it lets trainers monitor a learner's journey and, if necessary, change his or her course along the way to a secure arrival at the destination.

That's not merely a path. It's a trajectory. Gamification has an intentional direction. It meets the specific conditions of the voyage and voyager. And it exhibits adaptive tracking of its progress.

So, let's consider several stages in the learner's trajectory through a gamified training experience. In honor of my second company, where we developed many of these ideas, and which was called Rocketfuel Productions, I'm going to imagine this as a space voyage. And like every successful trip, it starts with a clear...

DESTINATION

The first rule of getting where you want to go is knowing where that is. I've been astonished by how many potential clients, amazingly enough, haven't really figured that out. They're not clear themselves about what they're trying to do, or even who they're talking to.

They need to take a step back and look at what they're really trying to get their training technology to do. Are they prequalifying potential employee candidates? Are they trying to get someone past a mandated compliance requirement? Are they trying to better develop existing employees? Or to retain them?

Know, and be able to articulate, precisely what skills or awareness or demonstrated knowledge the learner must "end the game" with. Then map out a route, through defined actions and challenge objects in the game play, that gives the player freedom to feel as if she is following her own impulses—while leading her reliably to the planned conclusion.

When someone comes to the gamified experience for the first time, there should be nowhere he can go except where you want him to go. In Web-based design, that's easy: you can arrange things so only one action icon "unlocks" at a time. The player completes that one, and then another unlocks. And so on.

We did that with a safety review for those construction-site drivers. When they opened the game, there was only one active icon. It opened a brief introductory video. When that had played, another action icon became available. It opened to a "walk-around" and safety check of their truck. Completing the walk-around opened a quiz next. And so it went, with each event or object that a student driver completed opening up one or more new ones to try.

Successful gamification requires that each step of play be essential to the whole journey. It should lead unmistakably to the following one. And it should provide just enough fuel and other resources to get there. More on those points below.

PLAY TO REALITY

Defining a successful trajectory depends on realism about conditions throughout the trip. Have you anticipated all the possible barriers? Could a crosswind blow up and knock the carefully planned navigation off-kilter?

To avoid being sent off course, your learner's trajectory through every module in the game needs to map as closely as possible to reality. There are two sides to this.

One reality is the organizational and occupational world that the training or awareness program is meant to prepare people for. I've had to tell some clients that their legacy training isn't working, because their corporate culture or philosophy just are not what they think they are.

A game scenario must match the organizational or workplace culture that it is training people for. If it doesn't, the dissonance gets in the way of the suspension of disbelief that's necessary to immerse yourself in any game—and certainly one your job, or another person's life, might depend on.

My favorite example of this is an organization we helped that had a mainly blue-collar workforce. Its better-educated HR department had prepared onboarding material written in good, clear, academic English. It advised trainees that they "should be prepared for confrontational situations," or some wording like that, on the work site.

Then we spoke to some actual employees as we were developing the module—and they gave us the reality. Verbatim. Foremen on work sites swore frequently, used bad language, and often berated junior employees. We put some of that language and behavior in the training module, and senior managers freaked out. "There's no way you can put that in a training module," they told me.

But that's exactly the problem. If you're training someone to work in the real world, perhaps on a work site with potentially life-threatening situations, you need your training material to actually reflect the truth of those settings—swear words and all.

The other reality that commands absolute respect is the audience's. Who are they? How do they learn best? Sometimes the question is quite literally: What language do they speak?

One client needed to validate employees' compliance with factory- specific legislative mandates. The company had prepared all sorts of written and text material. Then for compliance purposes, they also required employees to sign a document confirming they had read and understood the material they'd been presented with.

But these workers were mostly over forty-five years of age. Many of them were immigrants with little English. Most had very low literacy. How were they going to wade through legalese? They had barely any idea what was in the safety literature, let alone what they were being asked to sign. Some compliance!

In fact, the company to its credit realized it was courting some serious liability risks because its training was not effective, which is how they wound up talking to us.

Trainees need material to speak their language. The answer in the low-literacy workers' case was to let images carry as much of the story of the training game as possible. We helped the client and its legal team strip out as much text as possible and craft what was left so that it was both fully respectful of compliance requirements and still simple enough for our intended audience.

But here's an interesting and helpful fact: visual languages that work for low literacy, older laborers, work just as well for young educated Millennials.

We discovered this when we worked with the nurses' association I mentioned earlier. Its members were drawn almost entirely from the Millennial and Baby Boom generations—with not much in-between. When we tested learning modules on the association's members, we generally divided them into those two groups by age.

Amazingly to me, both groups responded equally well to material designed primarily for Millennial tastes. The impatient Millennial wants content delivered in a form that's intuitive to them, so they can move through it to the next thing as quickly as possible. The Baby Boomer is afraid of "breaking" something in the software if the task looks too complicated. They both want it easy.

It turns out their common language is visual. And it comes from their smartphone screen.

Have you ever noticed that there are quite literally hundreds of smartphone makes and models, plus at least two popular operating systems—Google's Android and Apple's iOS—and yet all their home screens look the same? Rows of squarish icons for apps.

And these days everyone has a smartphone. Millennials and Generation Zers won't leave the bedroom without theirs. My seven-year-old son doesn't have one yet, but he knows how to use one. So does my seventy-year-old immigrant dad. Their behavior with apps is exactly the same.

Except that if you gave my dad a training binder and told him to read it, he probably would. Even some younger Generation Xers like me might. But most Millennials and anyone from Generation Z will flat out refuse to even start a digital module if they don't think it looks like something on their smartphone.

A last aspect of playing to reality is technical. Speaking the language of today's trainee audience also means speaking to them from the cloud.

Nobody is tethered to a desktop computer any more. And no one of any age is happy being locked in a classroom for hours on end. Another reason we all have smartphones is that, thanks to affordable digital cell-phone data plans and the widening reach of free Wi-Fi hotspots, we can stay in touch pretty much 24/7 with all the resources of the Web wherever we happen to be.

Most of the time we use the power of our smartphone apps for things like checking our e-mail, finding out the driving conditions, and determining the ingredients for a recipe. We do it dozens of times a day from wherever we are at the moment: the café, the parking lot, the grocery store. But that also makes anyplace, own-pace access the dominant and most familiar way we reach out for and consume information.

Training and awareness material needs to speak to users in the same way. That means being always there in the cloud and speaking the visual language we all share, through devices that everyone carries with them.

IGNITION

The full "magic powers" of gamified training begin to appear when players immerse themselves enthusiastically in the game—emphasis on *enthusiastically*. For gamification to work hardest for the organizations that deploy it, it needs to give its users as much fun as possible even when playing is a job requirement.

If this paradox still leaves you uncomfortable, if you still think learning needs to hurt a little bit, I suggest you go back and have another look at what we talked about in chapter 3.

So, the moment of ignition is important. Users should *want* to start the module, not need to be *told* to start. Getting this to happen requires several things to work well at once, from the look of the training app icon sitting next to iTunes on their smartphones, to the premise of the opening screen.

And with enough imagination, this can be accomplished even for content that looks the least promising at first glance. Like accounting.

Seriously. Accounting is one of those functions that every organization and business needs, and every family budget would benefit from. The world absolutely needs good accountants. But sizzle? Sex appeal? Mystery or romance? Sadly, not so much.

So, when a professional accounting association asked us to help them deliver what they saw as a supplemental academic program for postsecondary students, blended with some marketing for the profession, we had to come up with something really creative. That's how the ACE Detective Agency was born.

A potentially eye-glazing training course became *The Accounted*, a gamified module with a story and graphic style inspired by noir detective movies of the Sam Spade era. It starred Ace, an intrepid investigator in a trench coat who needed players to help her with some finely honed accounting skills in order to solve a crime.

Ace successfully enticed a whole lot of young students to acquire and demonstrate some basic accounting skills. In fact, she turned out to be so popular that when we made *The Accounted* available to the public for a buck on Android and iPhone, it was downloaded more than 30,000 times. (It was also *The Accounted*—or at least the award we won for its execution and the conference I attended to pick it up—that introduced me to Nir Eyal's thinking.)

The cardinal sin of gamification is anything boring. Some lessons flow from that.

Most of us learn best visually. Use graphics, charts, and animation wherever possible. Avoid text. How many video console games or games on your phone do you play that have a lot of text? Exactly. There's a reason for that: text creates distance and disengagement. Images create intimacy. When we gamify, we're looking for intimacy. We want our content to get inside the players' defenses.

But there are other senses to stimulate. The kinesthetic and auditory are the easiest to evoke in gamified training design. Don't just allow players to click through to a new screen: make them drag and drop an icon. Give them an auditory cue or reward, a chord of music or a burst of applause.

But above all, KISS: "Keep it simple, Stupid." That's good advice for all types of communication. But for content that's going to be delivered via the Internet, there is an especially powerful evolutionary reason to heed it.

The Internet has changed mightily since the first pioneers communicated awkwardly in text, with special hand-typed codes to make sure messages went where they were intended. The invention of the World Wide Web, and graphic user interface browsers, like Chrome, Firefox, and Safari, freed most users from having to know anything at all about the technical side of the Internet.

Soon the Internet may fade even further from our conscious awareness. Google's chairman and ex-CEO Eric Schmidt, who knows a thing or two about Internet trends, told the World Economic Forum in Davos, Switzerland, that for most users "the Internet will disappear."

What he meant was that the Internet, as a medium that we need to think about, the way we think about the cell-phone network when we place a call, will disappear because we will never need to think about it at all. It will simply be there.

"There will be so many IP addresses, so many devices, sensors, things that you are wearing, things that you are interacting with," Schmidt told the Davos Forum, "that you won't even sense it. It will be part of your presence all the time."

Tech writer David McGillivray has taken this insight even further: "We'll gradually start to forget that devices [like phones or tablets] are even separate objects," he predicts. "Interfaces won't have edges, to the point where we'll eventually consider the interface as the experience, devoid of device, rather than simply graphics on a screen."

Today, digital designers worry about "cross-browser and cross-device compatibility," McGillivray says. "This complexity will be intensified as we consider the almost infinite malleability of the future interface."

And as devices disappear, he warns, designers will need to finely distill the content that users see. Text will need instant and razor-sharp legibility. "Perhaps we'll get to a place where type is rarely used," he thinks, when almost *all* content will be conveyed in icons.

It's not important how far down that visionary road the technology takes us. What matters is to understand the direction. Trainers can rely less than ever on the box that goes around their content. They need to think harder than ever about how that content appears to the learners they want to engage.

FUEL

Igniting blastoff is only the start of the voyage. You need to keep learners stoked for the full trip. And once again, it's the pleasure of play that keeps people motivated through the serious business of learning. It's "work" that doesn't feel like work.

The reason it doesn't feel like work is because of brain chemistry. Whenever you exert some effort in anticipation of a goal, and then earn a reward for accomplishing it, your brain releases a little burst of dopamine that floods its feel-good sensors.

Good game design—whether for entertainment or training—creates a continuous flow of challenges and successes that trigger this dopamine response. Expertly done, these create a chain of pleasure bursts that almost force someone to carry on exploring the next pleasure-inducing learning object in a gamified module. This is what we mean by making learning addictive. It almost is.

In gamified training, we use basically two types of rewards: points and badges. Points are a running tally of a person's activity and progress through the module. Badges are awarded for completing a particular section, quiz, or challenge. We accompany each with its own musical effect for that auditory stimulus.

This aspect of effective gamification demands as much art and psychology as it does logic. The pacing of each challenge and reward has to be just right. You want players to experience *just enough frustration* to give them the optimal dopamine hit when they master the challenge and receive a reward.

Facebook, as Nir Eyal has pointed out, understands this perfectly. It has built that just annoying enough half-second delay into the way its app loads on your phone. Everybody thinks the problem is with his or her phone. It's not. They're elevating your anticipation. Who has reacted to my last post? How many notifications will I see?

And badges, we've discovered, serve a second function in addition to providing that dopamine reward trigger. They provide a useful interruption in the user's progress. That way, players don't feel as if they're doing a hundred-question exam, even if they really are.

It's a fine line. And honestly some of it is weirdly arbitrary, but true nonetheless. Take quizzes or puzzle games, for example. After years of experimentation, we discovered that, for whatever reason, if you have to answer fewer than eight questions, it feels as if you haven't done enough. More than eight, and it seems like it's too long. That's why when my teams build a quiz into a learning module, right at that eight-question mark, it plays a little game-over music, dismisses itself, gives you a badge, and shows you the points you've earned.

Another fact of human psychology is that we're more motivated by the fear of losing something than we are by the prospect of gaining something of the same value. We'd rather forego making a dime than lose a nickel. Gamification leverages our different responses to loss and reward to keep learners more deeply engaged with content.

For example, when a player completes a task successfully, he earns twenty-five reward points. But when he makes a wrong response, he faces a five-point penalty. We've found that delivers just the right amount of aversive sting, while it allows most players to keep adding to their point total, even if they only get half of the answers right.

I'll have much more to say about the value of reward points and badges in the next chapter. In many ways, these two features are the secret sauce that make gamification a breakthrough in human resources and training productivity.

But to do that work, points and badges can't be indifferent to a player's actions. They can't be handed out just for moving through a module, the way loyalty reward points are earned for every purchase. That's phony gamification.

For real gamification, rewards need to reflect a learner's actual performance on tasks relevant to the training objective. To earn badges—and the dopamine burst they release—a player needs to complete a task or level correctly.

But even "addicted" learners want to take a break from time to time.

Rather than allow motivation to run out of gas, the best gamified training also lets users stop for a while and start again later.

That's a big difference from some e-learning platforms. With those, you can find yourself partway through a seventy-page course segment, and if you try to take a break, it pops up a warning. "Are you sure you want to leave? Because if you leave, you can never come back. You have to start over again."

At Rocketfuel, we learned very early the essential importance of the "pause and save game" function in entertainment gaming, and we were one of the first to implement it in gamified training. "Pause and save" is what lets you play a portion of a video game and then back out, leave, come back, and play it some more.

Let's face it, we're all a little ADD these days. We've got WhatsApp, Messenger, our social media apps, and continuous incoming e-mail alerts. It may be terrible for us to multitask, but we all do it as a matter of survival.

Smartphones encourage the habit. We go into an app for something—maybe a recipe—and use that app for a while. Then we leave and go on to the next app, to call an Uber or check the news. On average, we spend less than two minutes at a time on most public websites.

That's just how people natively seek out information in the age of the always-on Web. But because users are coming in and out so frequently, a lot of those apps have to be able to save their state when a user leaves, and return to it when their user calls them back up.

Gamified training plays to that reality. Players can dip in, break away, and come back to it just as they do with all the other tasks and searches in their daily lives. As a result, we see training moments becoming part of life moments.

We know that gamified training infiltrates people's non-work lives this way because we can see it in the tracking data that gamification provides. One of our higher-education partners, looking to train the next generation of physicians, had 192 people in its program. We watched them log in to their training game site 3,000 times. That means an average trainee logged in and engaged with the material more than 15 times.

We saw identical take-up in a large financial institution that was rolling out new customer-facing branding. It needed to bring 4,000 employees up to speed on various dimensions of this important change. Those employees logged in to the awareness game roughly 60,000 times—again, about 15 times each.

In that case, the "pause and save game" feature unlocked another capability of gamification: staged release of game elements. The financial firm released new game tasks featuring different dimensions of its rebranding initiative—the brand story, the company's presence in communities, the voice of the customer, and so on—over several months.

This could all have been unlocked at once. Instead, the end of each phase of the game "teased" the one coming up next with a message like, "Watch your e-mail or the corporate intranet for the next set of challenges." We actually got IT support requests asking when the next part of the game was coming out!

RANGE

The equation here is simple: the lighter our load, all other things being equal, the further we go. It's true of cars and pickup trucks, airplanes, and hikers. And learners.

Which is why I'm still amazed at the number of companies and organizations that load their complete employee manual, for example, up on the Web and expect learners to wade through it. Worse, they think that's interactive. This is bad for learning and a bad investment for the organization.

That kind of bulk content is text-heavy. It's boring and time-consuming. And it's almost impossible to track someone's progress through the information—let alone how much of it they absorb.

You can throw everything at a learner that you think she might *possibly* want to know, even when the great majority of it isn't critical. Or you can identify that fraction of the material that she absolutely *needs* to know. Then you reveal it to her as needed in a cognitive sequence designed to carry her forward most efficiently on a learning trajectory.

An example might be core safety knowledge. What is going to hurt workers? Visualizing those threats for learners is probably more urgent than introducing them to company history, for example.

You can always make that and all the rest available a click away in a resource library. That's a particularly valuable approach when there's a legislated compliance mandate involved.

In the case of our medical client, for example, there were 295 pages of legal clauses that the association's members were supposed to be generally aware of. That would stop most learners in their tracks right there. We broke it down into critical sections and must-knows. We focused on those in the gamified activities. But we also made the rest of the legal material available for people to check if they wanted to find out more. We even guided users who wanted that extra depth to the most relevant sections of the law.

But this is where HR and training professionals may need to up their game. They need to be able to scour their legacy and current content for what's most critical. In my experience, that's about 25 percent of what's in their library. Then they'll need to concentrate that into the most visually "legible" and easily-grasped "byte-size" elements. These must be served to learners the same way that Amazon makes its inventory logistics so efficient with just in time delivery.

This isn't easy. There have been a few organizations we've been unable to work with. We'd like to. They're nice people. But they don't know their own content well enough to prioritize the essential 25 percent. They're not ready or willing to rethink their habitual storytelling. Unfortunately, they may never be able to access the productivity gains that gamification energizes by refining content to lighten the learner's load.

Time is money. If you have 5,000 employees—as some of our clients do—and they're each spending five hours on an awareness module that could take them an hour, how much money have you lost?

And how many learners dropped out, at least mentally, long before the five hours were up, and learned less than they needed?

COURSE CORRECTIONS

Drawing on that old idea of the "choose your own adventure" book—where you could read alternative storylines with different endings—gamified training gives players the feeling that they're making choices. But that's not quite the reality. In fact, each of those choices is tightly tailored to carry learners through a necessary part of their trajectory.

But just creating a branching experience to give players the illusion of choice isn't ideal, because it has no dynamic feedback mechanism to tell when a learner is wandering off course.

Gamified learning watches every move and bakes in course-correction opportunities. It takes advantage of responsive digital technology to assess each trainee's individual progress through a module in real time. Then it can direct him automatically to a next task precisely selected for his state of readiness.

Players who already know the material zip right through. Someone who's having trouble with a section may be redirected to some remedial tasks, or she can choose— really choose!—to replay the particular game actions she's struggling with.

Of course, that's not all. We've all been told since we were kids that practice makes perfect, but who ever wanted to practice? The key to getting that learner to do something over and over? Make the experience not suck. Make it engage the imagination and those dopamine triggers.

Bring the arcade to the office.

PAYLOAD

A gamified learning trajectory delivers multiple payloads even before the journey is complete.

Application programming interface (API) connected software is widely available from a range of third-party suppliers. It allows data to flow seamlessly, securely, and in real time from wherever learners are engaged with a game, to an organization's enterprise software architecture. From there it can be delivered to any device dashboard that administrators or the C-suite customarily use for their data display.

Trainers and managers can follow trainees' progress through gamified modules in as much detail as they're curious about. They can monitor player advancement through training elements and note when learners need a course correction. Plus, of course, they can see each player's aggregate record in detail after they complete the module—as well as how any one or all metrics of interest might compare to those of any other individual who has used the module.

The immense wealth of new information that this data stream makes available is truly gamification's breakthrough advantage for HR managers and training staff. It's where I'll turn next, in chapter 6.

CHAPTER 6

DEEP SCORING

I'm passionate about what I do because I've seen firsthand how it can change a person's attitude toward learning from one of bored obligation to genuine enthusiasm. That's exciting to see and to help make happen.

But when I'm meeting with a client for the first time, more often than not they want to talk about ROI—return on investment. In the training, awareness, and assessment space, I tell them, they need to be thinking about the *I*-ROI: the *information* return on their training investment.

Just as I'm passionate about seeing someone become genuinely enthusiastic about learning, I'm equally passionate about clients' I-ROI. That's because I know that gamification wins hands down over competing teaching technologies. It is the key reason that gamification breaks through existing productivity ceilings in human resources and training functions.

Traditional teaching models, based on x number of hours of exposure to course material plus a test, are prone to failure from start to finish. Boring content delivery and information overload create unmotivated learners. Formal exams produce unreliable assessments of what they really know.

Gamified training is both more disciplined and more creative. It taps the unmatched motivation of learners' imaginative engagement in game action. It also allows trainers and HR managers an unparalleled—for the price—ability to actually "see what employees are made of" in reality-based scenarios. This is *deep scoring*. It is what unlocks gamification's powerful, affordable potential to reveal new insights.

Deep scoring is a breakthrough in value and productivity for in-service training. But it can pay off even more in the arena of preemployment qualification.

Author and leadership-development consultant Michael Watkins reports, in his book *The First 90 Days*, that "the break-even point where new hires add more value than they have consumed, is usually 6.2 months." That is, an average company needs to retain an average hire for at least 6.3 months to recoup its investment in recruiting that employee. For employees with higher recruitment costs, the retention time to recover them all is obviously longer.

And that's assuming the employee works out.

Bad hires are even more expensive. Best case, a bad hire sinks the entire cost of recruiting an individual—and paying him as long as he lasts—with no value recovery at all. The worst case? The employee makes a major mistake that incurs a significant liability, even personal injury or death.

Let me tell you about one organization that has relied on face-to-face interviews to assess employee competence. Gamified assessment raised a bright red flag over one new hire who had aced the in-person interview. Shortly thereafter, that employee's unsanctioned actions caused the organization tens of thousands of dollars in liability for property damage. Similar mistakes by employees who passed in-person assessments cost that organization $50 million a year across its global operations.

Deep scoring through gamified assessment can reduce the costly risk of bad hires.

THE TROUBLE WITH TESTING

Traditional testing and examinations—especially the formal kind with a clock running and a proctor watching—are not ideal, because they don't always deliver what they promise. Those kinds of examinations may be required by legislation or accrediting agencies for compliance purposes. But as a way of assessing knowledge, skills, or awareness, they have serious limitations.

At its best, a completed test form is a single data point. It's a summary of the test taker's current responses during one particular hour, or whatever time it took them to take the test, on one particular day.

Or at least of *someone*'s responses. Among its other weaknesses, conventional testing is vulnerable to substitute test takers. I've had clients tell me that they face a significant problem with employees or candidate workers who evade taking written tests through a variety of means. Some persuade friends or pay coworkers to take tests for them. One employee, an immigrant with poor language skills, had his son sign off on a compliance document that he couldn't read. Another pulled over just before he drove into the company yard and raced through a required online test—by pure guesswork—with his laptop tethered to his phone. (He was exposed later when he tripped up over some direct questions from a supervisor).

Even when it is the intended learner and not a ringer taking the test, set-piece exams are unreliable reflections of what someone knows. Maybe her baby was up all night, and she had no sleep before the test date. Maybe he has the flu.

Or maybe she's one of the many people who suffer from acute test anxiety: higher levels of debilitating stress *just because she's being tested*. Or the related problem: self-defeating learned helplessness that comes from convincing yourself that you do badly on tests, and so you do.

But even when someone has shown up fresh, rested, and full of confidence, he usually has less trouble with some questions and more with others. Some questions he stews over, and some he answers almost without having to think about them. Yet a completed exam form reveals practically nothing about which answers the learner has down and which he struggled over.

In other words, a multiple-choice test at the end of a video might not be a true indicator of who an employee or potential hire really is—or of her potential contribution or risk to an organization.

DEEP, WIDE, AND GRANULAR

Deep scoring produces a much wider spectrum of potential

insights into individuals and even entire work forces more than traditional testing and examinations. It can reveal much more granular, unguarded insights into individual personalities and aptitudes.

It can even expose surprising weaknesses in organizations beyond what's going on in their HR function. In fact, I warn my clients that they should be prepared to uncover things about their companies or practices through gamified assessment that neither of us could have anticipated, and which might not always be comfortable.

A key reason for that deeper insight is the comfort and engagement that users experience when they're in a gamified training environment. The emotional game state is one of "intense, optimistic engagement," as Jane McGonigal described it. It's a state of willing involvement in the game activity in which people are simply more likely to respond reflexively, authentically, and without calculation.

That opens new vistas for interrogation. Gamification allows designers to thread assessment phases—quizzes or questions—throughout game-play activity. Their prominence can be adjusted, from the subtle to the obvious, depending on the situation. (More below on why you might want to do this.) But from the standpoint of delivering the most accurate assessment, the ideal test is the one that leaves people unaware they're even being tested.

In a project we worked on recently, each chapter of the learning module contained a variety of tasks. Although players were told ahead of time that the gamified module would form part of their skills assessment, no one knew which two of the eight tasks in each chapter were being scored differently. They were actually the "exam."

Since players do not feel as if they're being tested, there is no acquired anxiety. No learned helplessness. Just authentic, honest, in-the-moment responses.

And that's not counting all the other information that gamification generates. Good gamified training tracks when people first try to log in. It detects whether they immediately begin playing and how often they have logged in since that first time. It knows what time of day people are engaging with which training module. At breakfast? At work? On their lunch breaks?

Web-based gamified training tracks in real time what sections of content learners have completed, and what points and badges they've earned. (More on those in a moment.) It can tell administrators, question by question, where people have answered right away and correctly, and where they've had to pause and think. It can tell whether they stop to read a patch of critical text, or just glance and click through. It identifies the questions where they took a stab at an answer and then second-guessed themselves. It tracks where they needed to go looking for guidance in the library of additional information.

Games also track players' *dis*engagement. We know when someone stops tapping on an object and when his screen has timed out.

At the end, you get a tangible and rich set of results that tell you much more about the employee than you would ever get from traditional testing, e-learning modules, or e-learning plus an exam.

Plus, of course, all that knowledge can be viewed either individually or aggregated across work units or an entire employee corps. And the raw data can be ported directly in real time back into whatever enterprise dashboard the organization uses.

Continuously tracking all learners' game activity tells administrators when members of a group start the training game. That's when they're most likely to be receptive to new information—providing potential opportunities to step up the training intensity during those windows of time.

Or the same activity tracking can expose training content that's not working. After a new module has been played by enough users, for example, I can tell a client, "Your users are dropping out of your module on average after thirty-two minutes, then they pick it up again later. At that point, they're in chapter 4. So, we may need to look at that. Chapter 4 may be too complex."

Similarly, say everyone playing the game consistently gets one element wrong. Maybe three-quarters of a group of trade apprentices fail to spot a known risk element in a construction scene. That could suggest that the training around that threat isn't being effective.

POINTS AND BADGES

But back to those points and badges. It's time we drilled down a bit more deeply into them, because they are critical to effective deep scoring. But they're also often misunderstood—even among some self-styled gamifiers.

People who haven't really grasped the concept will say things like, "Gamification is more engaging because it gives people points and badges." Or they'll call points and badges "rewards for getting through the material."

Those statements are both partly true. But they're also a bit like comparing points and badges to the lipstick on a pig, as nothing more than distraction from the unlovely reality. A spoonful of sugar to make the medicine of school work go down.

They completely miss the most important thing about these features of gamified learning.

Yes, points and badges are rewards. Players accumulate points as they move through in-game challenges and quizzes. They win a badge when they complete a section or subject—usually with a bit of digital hoopla attached. And yes, those regular rewards definitely contribute to maintaining that dopamine cycle that I described in the last chapter, to make learning continuously addictive.

But points and badges aren't enough on their own to keep users engaged. At best, they're one part of a holistic game experience that includes a narrative, a setting, and a trajectory, all designed and visualized to work together to create an irresistible invitation to the imagination. When it all works, you get a learning experience that can almost claim to be a minor gamification hit, like *The Accounted*.

Much more importantly, thinking of points and badges as *just* rewards overlooks their much larger vital role in true gamified training. If activity tracking is one part of the deep scoring data bounty that gamification provides to administrators, points and badges are the other half. Each one has a tangible tie in to a learning objective.

Properly designed, and tied to performance in specific game tasks along the learner's trajectory, point counts don't just follow progress through a training module. They provide another indicator of skill or awareness gained.

We've used points in different projects to reveal everything from academic knowledge for course credits to a player's psychological profile assessment. They can be designed simply to test a player's cognition and recall, or to create and mine altogether new data—as we did when we challenged one client's players to "get a fellow employee to tell you what they don't like about their job, and earn points!" (Yup. It worked, too!)

Points accumulate as people move through a module's tasks. Players earn badges when a module and its embedded quizzes and hidden assessments are completed. Together, points and badges tell us the level of difficulty a learner has surmounted—and something about the effort she expended to get there.

DEEPER INSIGHTS

Good gamification modules are tailored closely to their audience and purpose, as I said in the last chapter. But they also present every user with the same playing field and challenges, then follow everyone's play with continuous screen- and click-tracking. That also makes it possible to benchmark each section of a learning module by how well a skilled or knowledgeable player would perform on those challenges, tasks, or quizzes.

We've done that quite often with clients. Before a module gets released to its trainee audience, we'll have some of their existing top-performing employees in that subject area play the game. As they do, we track their point totals earned in each section of the game, along with their badge accumulation.

This creates something like the par score for each hole on a golf course: a reference point for each knowledge element. Now that you know what the pro can do, you have something to compare the learner, job applicant, or credential seeker to. It can shed a vital light not just on high-performing staff, but also on those who might pose an actual enterprise risk.

For one client, we developed a gamified module to increase their employees' awareness of protocols for certain customer-facing exchanges. The scenario involved listening to a scripted call-center exchange and then answering some questions. A vice president signed off on the script.

Almost as soon as we released the module, however, I got a note from one of the frontline employees saying, "No, that's wrong! They gave the customer the wrong information!" Then the note listed all the reasons why the exchange modeled in the game was wrong. It turns out, the script that the executive approved had contained wrong information. They were literally teaching incorrect content! I told the client that everyone who'd written an e-mail calling attention to the potentially costly mistake deserved a raise.

More routine anomalies pop out when data can be read at any or all of the individual, team, division, or enterprise levels, depending on a game's audience.

Usually, you get the typical distributions of performance around the average. Then you get the individuals who are right off the map. Take a client I've mentioned before in the heavy equipment space.

We completed a module assessing employee awareness of safe operating practices. A complete score was 7,000 points and a certain number of badges.

When we reviewed how its operators had played, we found most of them had reached the 7,000-point completion threshold. A few keeners had reached 8,000 or 9,000 points. They'd gone back and played a few sections twice. A handful of people were way down there and obviously hadn't even finished the module.

Then there was one guy with 15,000 points. He'd gone through the entire module, start to finish, *twice!* That just didn't make sense. Our stuff is good, but it's usually not *that* crazy good.

When I flagged him to the client, HR had him in for a talk. It turned out he hadn't absorbed three-quarters of the hands-on training he'd received before he played the assessment game. He had no clue. So, he played the game twice to learn the information he didn't comprehend in the course. In turn, the company took special measures to extend his training and made sure he was fully comfortable with his job's safety requirements before they sent him out to work.

The guy also had no clue where in the game he'd been tested. Or even *that* he'd been tested. Yet that scoring anomaly might have just saved his life—or saved the company from having a guy out on worker's compensation for six months because he tripped over a misplaced hose.

But deep scoring can also expose unexpected strengths. The ability to monitor people's performance across all the situations they encounter in a gamified training experience can also identify candidates for additional responsibility. Looking over the shoulder of players, administrators can often spot the ones who are most likely to repay an organization's investment in their development

When I spoke later with the client whose problem operator had marked himself for attention by doubling the safety module's completion score, I learned something else. The client had invited some other top-scoring, but not over-the-top, operators in for interviews, too. Based on the above-average initiative those employees showed in those conversations, several were now in line for management positions.

STORY FIRST, DATA SECOND

Reports on all this deep scoring data can appear in whatever format provides the greatest value for the organization. Usually there are at least two levels of record visibility: individual and aggregate. But some cautions are in order.

One is simply the risk of generating *too much* data. Managers already receive a flood of data from their organization's many systems: cash flow, logistical, customer-facing, internal, and external. More and more executives are finding that they struggle to make sense of it all. There's even a growing job category of "big data storytellers," people who can draw meaning from all those raw numbers.

That's backwards, in my view.

Generate data to suit your need; don't let your needs be captive to the data. First, identify *what information matters most* to the organization about its personnel, its members, or other client populations, as well as their knowledge. What is the story administrators are looking for? Then, pinpoint the specific queries that will reveal that critical information. Good gamification bakes in assessment objects that assemble the right data.

Good gamification providers present the storytelling data that training modules generate in whatever format is most useful to their clients. Reports should bring the most valuable insights from such deep-scoring exercises to the surface and foreground. They should make key comparisons quickly apparent. The two most popular formats, for example, show ranked individual performance and a comparison of individual performance against the whole playing population.

Top-line data, on module completions and overall performance, should also be available at a click on your smartphone. This isn't hard. And it's helpful when the CEO corners you in the elevator and asks you how that whole "gamification thing" is going!

I do have one reservation about how some organizations want to present results from gamified assessments.

While HR staff have a reason to want to know performance rankings—sometimes called "leaderboards"—I'm generally not a fan of disclosing them to the ranked participants. In any group, three or four top performers will always own the leaderboard, leaving everyone else to feel that top spot is unattainable. That's hardly motivating. In fact, there's a shaming aspect to it that can be a powerful disincentive. I urge clients not to use this approach.

There is an exception to that rule. In sales, where competition is part of the occupational culture, I think leaderboards can be leveraged to advantage.

A better way to approach this is what Nike does in its consumer apps for recreational consumers. It benchmarks individuals against an anonymous comparison peer group. So, you might be told, for instance, that "you are in the thirtieth percentile among people in your age range and gender in your city."

This kind of group benchmarking can be valuable within large organizations, too.

We had one client with numerous divisions. The organization asked us to develop a module for an internal marketing campaign. Halfway through the three-month campaign, a senior vice president discovered that one division wasn't participating. After some inquiry, they discovered that the same division's staff typically did not participate in many company initiations they really should have attended.

Suddenly, the division's vice president had some explaining to do. Head office was calling into question all its internal protocols and policies.

THE LIMITS OF FAIR PLAY

As gamification has developed, its ability to deliver penetrating insights about individuals and groups has become increasingly powerful. Those insights can help reveal whether an individual has been hired in the wrong part of an organization, may already have his eye on the door, or has the makings of a twenty-year employee.

Two people may be equally qualified by typical HR standards. They have the same number of years' experience, similar backgrounds, and interview equally well in person. Which is the better hire?

An individual's game play, her pace through a module, the tasks she chooses first, the number of mistakes she makes, which tasks she replays—all reveal certain personality traits. They can all help determine a candidate's "fit score" for a particular role in an organization.

Mike may be awesome at focus and attention; he can pick out minute mistakes and likes to check the documentation before he acts. Manuel is quick and decisive, but only scans information and misses details. Joe is timid in his actions, while Sarah is bold in hers. It's all revealed in the game, and it all comes out in deep scoring.

The key signal can be something quite small. Should someone who takes three tries to enter his e-mail correctly, for example, be relied on to enter health or financial data accurately?

The limits of what gamification can tell us in this area are still being explored. Once players are in that game state of "intense, optimistic engagement" with the scenario, and barely aware that they are being tested, there are opportunities to widen the scope of what they're asked to reveal about themselves.

In addition to elements oriented to core workplace or compliance requirements, some clients are beginning to ask us to include psychology-based questions in game scenarios. These can be very simple. A question like, "What's your favorite color?" for instance, may give clues to the test taker's temperament. Questions can also be more invasive or more subtle.

A game could include player choices involving unhealthy activities such as eating junk food, smoking, or skipping exercise, for example. Those could later be interpreted to indicate similar impulses in real life.

Ethical assessments might be embedded in game situations devised specifically to find red flags regarding employees who could pose compliance liabilities. A financial institution, for example, might be very interested in knowing how applicants for a position handling customers' funds respond when a game situation gives them an opportunity to cheat a little!

In fact, gamification's potential to disarm players' emotional and psychological defenses is so great that it should raise ethical questions of its own. It's not entirely for nothing that some parents worry about how much time their kids spend at the arcade or gaming online, and what they reveal when they do.

When the power of the arcade is brought into the office, it needs to be done responsibly.

Trainers, HR managers, and gamification designers all need to think carefully about how intrusive to be in taking advantage of this new technology's Trojan-horse potential. It's one thing to watch over the shoulder of a player as she reveals workplace-relevant aspects of herself. It would be another to take advantage of her game state of mind to probe for, say, unrelated political beliefs or clues to ethnicity or sexual orientation.

A different ethical question comes up when tests are mandated for individual or organizational compliance purposes.

Let's say health professionals need to be familiar with the current legislation in their field—the case of our client nursing association. The applicable law mandates that nurses demonstrate that familiarity and determines the questions they must answer correctly in order to do so. Accreditations, jobs, and livelihoods ride on the result.

Those critical mandated questions can certainly be presented in a gamified setting. But they should be clearly identified as ones that *count formally* toward the player's legal accreditation.

For example, they may display a different color when they unlock and become available to play. Or players might get a written warning: "You're about to take a test item. If you want to leave now and do more test prep, you should do so." A truly proactive gamified implementation would require that users confirm that they've read the warning before they're allowed to continue.

Other clients that wish to apply a more formally structured examination attach it to the end of a training module. When users complete the last object in the training, their final click takes them to the first test page.

A TEAM SPORT

Good gamification does two things seamlessly. One: it has to ignite the player's interest and emotional engagement in the module's game, and maintain that engagement to the end. And two: it has to track the player's responses minutely at every stage of the game, and report that data in a way that's intuitively most useful to administrators.

That, quite honestly, is a tall order. An organization may know the content it wants to convey through and through. Gamifying it effectively will still take multiple proficiencies.

The content needs to be prioritized and sequenced into a trajectory. A game scenario concept has to be conceived, and the content scripted into it. Action and assessment objects need to be developed within the script. In-game challenge elements like "This or That" choices, or "Find the Missing Word" games, need to be built. And finally, all of that needs to be programmed into a visually engaging user experience that plays smoothly across a variety of browsers and devices—while constantly linking to enterprise servers with real-time tracking data.

Most corporate human resources or training units simply don't have a sufficiently wide suite of skills to accomplish all this. That's why most organizations that choose to leverage the enormous HR productivity gains of gamification find their most cost-efficient option is to access an outside resource.

But as I've hinted in these pages, not everything that's marketed as gamification deserves the name. Nor can services trading on the term without really understanding it deliver fully on gamification's promise.

That's a double pity. It deprives organizations of gamification's true benefits. And the inevitably disappointing results from faux gamification threaten to discredit the most important new development in training technology in a couple of generations.

How to tell the real thing from the pretenders and win big? That will be the topic of chapter 7.

CHAPTER 7

READY TO PLAY?

—

The adoption of any new technology in the marketplace follows a regular pattern.

A few early adopters break new ground. The earliest pioneers often fail to make the new technology work and may even go broke. But soon enough those who master it reap large rewards. As a now-proven practice spreads to additional sectors, the most competitive players in each also adopt it—and see their competitive position strengthened. Over time, the new technology becomes the standard. And those who didn't adopt it soon enough are forced out of the marketplace.

Right now, gamification sits somewhere between the second and third stages of adoption. The technology is proven. Early adopters are seeing the first real gains in human resources and training productivity in a quarter century. And those gains are now catching attention across a widening spectrum of economic and organizational sectors. Gamification is driving better, faster, and more informative training and assessment functions in finance, health care, construction, and energy, to name only a few sectors.

That's both a good and a bad thing. The good is that a growing number of organizations are poised to capture the many benefits of gamification. The bad is that many organizations still don't really know what they're looking for. Meanwhile, far too many providers are taking advantage of that uncertainty by passing off inferior services as gamification.

Eventually gamification will also become an industry standard in human resources and training. Professionals in the field will know their way around its benefits and requirements, as well as most of them know their presentation software today.

Meanwhile, it's a bit of a wild west out there. As different providers have developed various rudimentary versions of today's state-of-the-art gamification, they've applied almost as many names to their approaches: "multimedia," "edutainment," "serious games." There are more than 650 learning management platforms on the market today. HR and training managers are inundated with buzzwords and high-tech offerings.

Countless small independent companies offer instructional design. Many claim to offer gamified training. Most don't.

In this environment, some HR managers go into paralysis. They rationalize doing nothing by saying they'll wait for the market to shake out. The risk is that, while they're waiting, their more forward-leaning competitors are already reaping gamification's benefits. They risk becoming one of those organizations that waits too long and gets left behind.

Other managers do the equivalent of closing their eyes and picking a provider out of a hat. Then they expect that vendor to be the magic bullet that solves all further challenges and meets their most inflated expectations.

In this chapter, I'd like to provide some clarity. I want to help you cut the head-spinning array of great-sounding offerings down to a manageable short list of candidate vendors whose platforms or services are clearly relevant to your training and HR objectives. And then I want to help you find the provider that will actually unlock those real productivity gains.

HOW TO ASSESS THE QUALIFICATION OF A VENDOR

The most obvious first question to ask about any vendor in this space is: Do they know what gamification really is? You now do. Do they?

Can they say how gamification is different from the offerings above and below it in the knowledge-transfer technology hierarchy? Can they place it between e-learning platforms (which lack imaginative engagement and "smart" assessment) and physical simulators (more immersive, but orders of magnitude more expensive)?

Can the vendor volunteer the key elements of true gamification? There are four: engagement, trajectory, ubiquity, and data.

Recall the definition at the beginning of this book:

Gamification is the use of design and insights from video games in the organizational space to engage trainees on multiple devices as they follow a learning narrative to targeted outcomes, generating real-time assessment data. *Engagement*.

Structured game play advances them along a tailored learning and assessment trajectory to defined outcomes. *Trajectory*.

Material is available to users on demand, at any time or place via the cloud, and across multiple device platforms. *Ubiquity*.

Gamified training modules generate rich, real-time data, customized for administrative review at individual and aggregate scales. *Data*.

Each one of those aspects is important. Your provider should be aware of all four characteristics necessary to fully functional gamification and be able to explain clearly and convincingly how their offering addresses each one.

If their product is heavy on written words and tests, move on. If it's based on clicking through screens of static content, again, give it a pass. The same if its delivery is limited to the company network. Any one of those shortcomings should strike a provider from consideration.

Well-gamified content engages all the senses, especially the visual and kinesthetic. It's available wherever the learner is, in his own place and at his own pace, on his smartphone, tablet, or any other Web-connected device.

But even something that *looks* "gamier," that boasts points and badges and flashy art, may not be capable of delivering the benefits of the real thing. Do the points and badges clearly relate to performance metrics that matter to your company or organization? If they only reward someone's digital progress through the training content, they're largely meaningless gold stars.

And how will those metrics—and all the rest of the data embedded in a user's activity in the game module—get back to administrators? Does the vendor have a comprehensive understanding of API bridging, so that they can work with IT to smoothly stream tracking data to the enterprise's management systems in real time?

Just as important, how will that data appear to administrators? Data that drowns the user in spreadsheet cells is hardly useful. The vendor should be able to provide a user-friendly data dashboard that highlights the metrics most relevant to management goals. The dashboard should be able to do this at individual, aggregate, or subgroup—department, division—scales. And it should do it in real time. You should be able to e-mail the link to your

CEO so she can pop it up on her own device screen and see up-to-the-minute reports.

Don't accept a vendor who promises only a daily data dump. That's a recipe for data overload, generating no useful information.

If the vendor's answer to how their offering feeds back performance data to administrators is "leaderboards," that should be another red flag. In addition to their counterproductive influence outside inherently competitive workplace settings, these are just plain lazy. Leaderboards provide no granularity in the insights they provide into individual users' performances. They're shallow scoring, not deep scoring.

Which leads to another qualifying—or *dis*qualifying—question. Can the vendor's platform do deep scoring at all? Can it provide insights that differentiate job candidates by their fit and suitability for different roles in the organization?

Some vendors simply won't understand the question. They're focused only on moving someone through a body of content, perhaps to a compliance test on specified content. They won't see deeper insights into players' behavior or aptitudes as a part of their offering at all. They may use some gamification techniques. But they're also blind to at least part of its potential. Think twice.

ARE THEY READY FOR A RELATIONSHIP?

As important as *what* a vendor's product can offer is *how* they will interact with your organization. A provider may be able to promise "smart" gamification with plenty of tracking and readouts, but those features will only be as good as they are relevant to your organization's training or awareness goals. And only you know what those are.

A vendor should be able to explain how they will make sure that your company's objectives will lead their implementation of a gamified solution. This is where many providers—and clients—get their carts before their horses. A conversation shouldn't start with someone trying to sell you on a particular technology platform. It should start by determining whether a vendor has a plan for a creative partnership. Because that's what it needs to be.

The vendor should be able to articulate a clear, iterative, and well-practiced approach to gamifying your organization's unique training and assessment needs.

This should start with a discovery process. This is where the vendor asks *you*, the client, a lot of questions. They should be designed to understand both your organization's key goals and your trainees' contexts. Is the game audience highly literate or of low literacy? Are key workplace concepts abstract (accounting) or physical (construction safety)? Can the vendor help you become more specific and articulate about key awareness objectives or critical capacity benchmarks?

The next phase of generating compelling gamification is developing the learner's trajectory. What is the optimal sequence in which to introduce material? What are the critical assessment points? And how can those be woven together into a compelling, overarching game narrative? You need to work out the training or awareness "story" first. Only then can you identify the specific data that will be needed to demonstrate that it's been followed and absorbed.

The learner's trajectory and its assessment points should determine how a provider shapes your content. Any production cycle that begins before the trajectory is defined will more than likely waste money—at the very least. At worst, it could send the project off in entirely the wrong direction. It's the equivalent of pulling out of the driveway to cross the country without checking a map first. You may get there...eventually. But you'll spend a lot on gas and motels before you do.

Technical issues—what the actual delivery software platform will be, the protocols for data bridging back to the enterprise data system—should be the last thing in the vendor's development schedule. That's because they're usually resolvable with relatively generic, off-the-shelf solutions.

A vendor who pitches you on their "back end" before they have identified through discovery what your company actually wants to accomplish probably won't get it done.

A couple of considerations are important to keep in mind, though. Whatever platform and API the offering uses, it should *not create extra work* for the organization's IT department after implementation. And it must be inherently secure. There are numerous ways to accomplish this, but your vendor should be able to work smoothly with whatever level or flavor of data system you already have.

This highlights a sensitive point: the critical balance between what a vendor provides and what a client does, as they work together to create compelling gamified training objects.

Be wary of a vendor who promises to maximize the legacy value of existing content by jazzing it up with rewards, points, and badges. Simply posting huge amounts of existing content into an online dump isn't gamifying. It's e-boring. That content is important and can often be usefully repurposed—as video clips inside a game module, for instance. But it needs to be the foundation of the game, not its foreground.

Similarly, points and badges merely slapped onto reams of legacy content every few screens are empty awards. The vendor needs to join the client's subject-matter experts in an iterative discovery process to ensure that (a) only the most important stuff gets into the game and (b) any points and badges awarded truly differentiate users by performance on indicators that are valid for the training goal.

Like any creative relationship, this one can sometimes be fraught. Some organizations insist that their own staff can simply update their legacy content and give the gamifier a script to follow. That almost never works out well for either party.

Too often, the project bogs down because people don't really know what they're doing. Client staff haven't anticipated predictable technical issues such as character count, or narrative ones such as the sequence of actions and quizzes in the module. Half of the elements have to be sacrificed for one reason or another, with a big waste of effort and money.

Then, people being people, client personnel become personally attached to aspects of the gamification process that are beyond their professional competence—pacing of the game action, for example, where to locate menus on the screen, or how many questions to ask at one time. Soon, what should be easy steps in the process become bottlenecks.

When working with a gamifying service provider, it's more important for the HR or training professional to focus on her own content and subject-matter expertise. That's the part that no gamifier, not even the best, can know about when he has his first meeting with you. Yet at the end of the day, it's also the most important thing. It is the core body of knowledge that has to be mined, refined, and conveyed to learners in gamified form.

Human resources and training staff need to be the stewards of that knowledge. Their company or organization, the learner, and the gamifier are all counting on them to know what awareness is absolutely mission critical, and what is useful but not urgent background knowledge.

Which is more important for a credentialing body to know, for example: whether a midwife is aware of the proper name of the law that governs her profession, or whether she knows what to do when a baby presents in a breech birth?

The client company or organization is always the content expert and responsible for identifying its priorities. The gamifier provides the tools and creative collaboration to turn that content into story, then into game action, and finally into organization-relevant data.

A question that sometimes arises for clients at this point is: "OK, we're working together to create this new gamified thing, but *who owns it when we're done?*" The answer is really very simple. Anything a client brings into a project remains theirs. That absolutely includes all their original subject-matter content.

A vendor may employ either its own proprietary software or licensed software to implement a client's gamification. The ownership of that intellectual property similarly remains with the existing rights-holder.

Such intellectual property and copyright issues may be new to some training professionals, but they are routine in a wide variety of collaborative settings. Think copyrighted images of famous celebrities used in advertising. This should seldom present a problem in a relationship with a mature gamification vendor.

THE PART ABOUT MONEY

As much as good gamification leads to breakthroughs in training productivity and human resources insights, it still costs money. Senior budget-setting executives will always want to know how much it will cost and whether it can't be done cheaper.

Let's talk ballparks.

Gamification will always come in at a higher cost than e-learning platforms. It will reward that extra expense with greatly enhanced learner engagement, and vastly richer *I*-ROI—*information* return on investment. Getting-into-the-game projects will likely attract proposals starting at around $50,000. More elaborate and lengthy campaigns may reach up to $250,000 to $300,000. Another option that some providers may offer clients is to pay less for the learning module, but then pay a certain amount for each learner who uses it.

Some savings are possible where existing image or document assets can be repurposed in the gamified content. Making in-house subject-matter expertise available can also help contain costs. So can having in-house personnel contribute to copywriting and asset collection. Putting a little of the organization's own creative skin in the game that way can also help stoke internal enthusiasm for the finished product later.

Lastly, any HR or training practitioner who wants to delve more deeply into the key psychological and tactical dynamics that make gamified learning addictive should grab a copy of either of Jane McGonigal's two great books, *Superbetter* or *Reality Is Broken*. For more understanding of how to implement those dynamics in training material—or almost any other product or service, for that matter—be sure to check out *Hooked* by Nir Eyal.

CHAPTER 8

GAME ON!

—

Gamification is the first truly transformative innovation to appear in the training, awareness-building, and human resources space in more than a quarter century.

Compared to old-school classrooms and more recent enhancements such as presentation software and e-learning platforms, an office arcade delivers actual productivity gains and wide-ranging additional insights. And it does so at 1/1000th the cost of the last wave of transformative training technology: the immersive simulator.

These productivity gains are real. They come from more engaged and enthusiastic learners who absorb "byte-size" content material faster, retain it longer, and even elect to study on their own time. Additional gains come from players' strongly self-motivated, in-game repetition of sticking-point content and recourse to readily accessible library documentation. The result: faster time to greater improvement in performance and awareness.

Those gains in productive engagement with learning hold true across all age cohorts. But among Millennials and younger generations, gamification may be decisive as to whether an organization has a training and assessment capacity at all. Its presence can make the difference between a talented new hire who completes an onboarding assessment—and one who walks out after five minutes muttering something about "last-century" companies!

Gamification's deep scoring potential delivers a further huge boost to the productivity of HR and training functions. The ability to track players' progress through content material in real time, complete with hesitations and redos, opens up an altogether new level of personnel insight. It supports highly granular metrics for individual strengths and weaknesses for interests, risk profiles, position fit, and potential within an organization.

And these insights are more valid with gamification than ever before. Players' willing emotional engagement with gamified learning activity reduces the test anxiety and learned helplessness provoked by conventional high-stress assessment protocols. It encourages more authentic, in-the-moment responses that are more likely to accurately reflect a subject's actual knowledge, awareness, or skill level.

And yes, there's more.

Good gamification reports all that insight back to administrators, managers, and, should they want it, executive-level officers, in real time. It does so in reporting formats customized to the organization's goals. It can integrate that data seamlessly into existing enterprise systems through off-the-shelf third-party software. And it can do that with a degree of security at least as strong as the organization's own network boasts.

THE FOUR KEYS TO BREAKTHROUGH

What makes all this possible? The four keys to gamification's productivity breakthroughs are engagement, trajectory, ubiquity, and data.

Insights from the enormously successful entertainment gaming industry into how to secure and hold player engagement, applied to the organizational training and awareness sphere, make learning addictive and engaging.

Storytelling inspired by the same models, critically informed by organizational subject-matter expertise and content stewardship, creates learning trajectories that securely navigate learners to desired awareness objectives.

Device-agnostic delivery via the user's Web or mobile browser and the ubiquitous cloud, in a visual vernacular familiar to everyone who uses a smartphone—which is to say, pretty much everyone—breaks training free from the workplace. It encourages players to invite learning into their off-work "real" lives, giving it a privileged intimacy. This results in expanded time windows for learning—including unpaid time—and more authentic assessment responses.

Together, the three foregoing characteristics of gamification—engagement, trajectory, and ubiquity—enable the fourth—deep scoring, or data. The real-time flow of high-resolution insights, keyed to specific organizational goals, is what makes gamification a true breakthrough knowledge technology. For the first time, it brings insights formerly available only at high cost to a relative handful of corporations and agencies, into a price range that most companies and organizations can afford.

Coming from among the earliest of the Millennial generation, I may find these ideas to be more natural than some readers. I appreciate your sticking around through them!

But as familiar or novel as these ideas may be to you, I promise you that I wrote this book because I know just how powerfully they perform in organizational training and awareness. If you have ever stayed up later than you meant to, glued to your screen and keyboard or NES controller, you know what I'm talking about. And you can bet your pension that your next twenty- or thirty-something job candidate knows!

I have seen gamification deliver on these promises repeatedly. Training and assessment using next-generation techniques as outlined here in *Office Arcade* have shattered low productivity expectations for clients ranging from broad-shouldered construction and engineering companies to people-oriented health professions and financial-services groups.

They can do the same for your organization.

ACKNOWLEDGEMENTS

———

I want to thank my wife Jennifer for her love and support, in particular, since I decided to become an entrepreneur. It's been a long, difficult, and sometimes painful road to get to this point, and I couldn't have done it without her. To my sons Ethan and Malcolm, I hope this book one day acts as a reminder that through hard work and dedication, you can do whatever you want in this world.

I want to thank my parents Frank and Maureen for allowing me to spend hours on end playing video games on my Nintendo, Sega Genesis, PlayStation, etc. I'm sure it seemed like I was wasting my time, but all of those hours gaming really payed off. Special thanks to my sisters Daniela and Liana for helping out with the two player/co-op games.

I also want to thank all of the people who've helped me get our software company off the ground. Trajectory IQ would not be where it is today without the dedication of our staff, and the support of our clients, partners, and investors.

ABOUT THE AUTHOR

———

Born and educated in Alberta, Canada, JASON SURIANO is a digital, gaming, and Generation X native. Coming of age with the Internet, he saw that its most important insights would be about people, not technology, and therefore he studied humanities computing at university.

Jason cofounded his first company in 2008. Rocketfuel Productions Inc. is an award-winning educational technology company that works with such clients as engineering and logistics giant ATCO, Chartered Professional Accountants, Discovery Communications, and the Royal Tyrrell Museum of Paleontology. In 2013, he founded Trajectory IQ, the first gamified software designed specifically for corporate onboarding and awareness training.

Trajectory IQ provides unexpectedly entertaining, data-rich awareness and training solutions for professionals in HR, marketing, and a range of safety, customer service, and other operational areas.

Jason has also served as the Executive Director of the Alberta Information and Technology Council, and as Co-Chair of Communications for the Advertising Club of Edmonton.

Jason is available to organizations and conferences as a popular speaker on gamification's many benefits. For specific inquiries regarding gamification services, you can contact Trajectory IQ at hello@trajectoryiq.com